"Excellent historical and overall view of Kodály Method as originally conceived. Very useful chapters on scope and sequence of the Method as might be adapted for use in the American school system.,... Quite impressed with the Song Source Section, the section on pedagogical use of the songs, and the way in which the songs are categorized and presented in order of usability."

"This is the best book I have read on the Kodály Method. It is concise, simple enough to be read by either a music major or non-major. There is a wonderful list of songs in the back."

"An *excellent* contribution to the field. Obviously well researched. Knowledgeable, clear, concise, most helpful. . . . Thank you Ms. Choksy."

"Valuable little volume . . . gets at the major ideas beautifully."

"Excellent book—well organized—attractive, good *solid* reading. I am recommending it to my students as a 'must' for their future professional libraries."

"One of the best books I have encountered concerning both background and philosophy. Lesson plans are comprehensive, clear, and valuable. Fine collection of songs."

Lois Choksy's volume gives you an accurate description of the Kodály Method of music education—covering historical development in Hungary and its international spread; current use in Hungary; and uses and application in American schools.

This helpful, practical guide provides specific examples of lessons and of lesson planning. The author illustrates topical points with 158 songs organized precisely in the sequence of the Kodály Method.

The Kodály Method is appropriate for your students in elementary education, music education, and current music trends and methods.

Lois Choksy (Kodály Certificate, Franz Liszt Academy of Music, Budapest, Hungary) Member of the Supervisory Staff, Baltimore County Board of Education.

The Kodály Method

The Kodály Method

Comprehensive Music Education
from Infant to Adult

LOIS CHOKSY

105805

PRENTICE-HALL, INC., Englewood Cliffs, New Jersey

Library of Congress Cataloging in Publication Data

CHOKSY, LOIS.
    The Kodály method.

    1. School music—Instruction and study.
2. Kodály, Zoltán, 1882–1967. I. Title.
MT1.C537K6   372.8'73   73-18316
ISBN 0-13-516765-5
ISBN 0-13-516757 — 4 pbk.

© 1974 by Prentice-Hall, Inc.
Englewood Cliffs, New Jersey

Printed in the United States of America

10   9

PRENTICE-HALL INTERNATIONAL, INC., *London*
PRENTICE-HALL OF AUSTRALIA, PTY. LTD., *Sydney*
PRENTICE-HALL OF CANADA, LTD., *Toronto*
PRENTICE-HALL OF INDIA PRIVATE LIMITED, *New Delhi*
PRENTICE-HALL OF JAPAN, INC., *Tokyo*

To the memory of Zoltán Kodály

Contents

Foreword

In many parts of the world great numbers of music teachers are attempting to apply the pedagogical principles of the late Professor Zoltán Kodály in their own cultural environments. It is no exaggeration to state that people come to Hungary today from every corner of the globe to study the model in its place of origin. In this era of the superjet geographical distances have disappeared, and with this disappearance the only distances that still remain are the kind between people and people! In an age when one may travel without difficulty from one side of the earth to the other, people travel for a variety of reasons: some for tourism, others for entertainment or out of curiosity, still others simply because they have nothing better to do. In a completely different category are those travelers who undertake a journey to learn, to gain knowledge, to learn to teach.

Teaching today is not an easy job, and in the field of education even more difficult is the task of the music teacher who wishes to sow the seed of humanistic culture in future generations; to pass on the method of the Greek muse Musiké. Will they listen to him? Will they pay attention to his message? Can he exert an influence on the growing generation? All these are burning questions to the dedicated music teacher wherever he may live in the world. He deals with them because he feels a bit responsible for the changing of the world's face.

This responsibility is felt by the author of this book, my dear friend and colleague, Lois Choksy. She has transplanted her Hungarian observations into American soil, observations made first from a distance, then by close association, made first in theory, and later with much practical work. Her book gives valuable guidance to all who wish to be guided. It is an able and gifted adoption which encourages the reader to further accomplishments, polishing, and discovery.

The structure of the book is very clear, logical, and well organized, but it is not intended to replace any teacher's own personal work. The recipes are here, but a good cook is always needed to prepare a delicious meal. The Kodály Method is not an "instant" method, however simple it may seem if one only examines it superficially. Good method, devoted teacher, and responsive children . . . given the first two, can one doubt that the third component is easiest to get?

Warmest greetings to the reader from the other side of the ocean! Let us join hands. Perhaps we can still save the world. In any case, if we try to realize the guiding principle of Zoltán Kodály's life and to help people to "let music belong to everyone," we will have done what we could, and the after-ages cannot call us to account for our negligence.

Erzsébet Szönyi

Dean of the Faculty for Music
Education at the Franz Liszt
Academy of Music, Budapest

Vice-President of the International
Society for Music Education (ISME)

The Kodály Method

Introduction

Some years ago I was teaching a lesson about the violin to a first grade class. I had taken a violin into the classroom with me for demonstration purposes. I held it up and said, "Can anyone tell me what this is?" A youngster in the front row said, "It's a fiddle." "Yes," I said, "Its nickname is fiddle, but its real name is 'violin'—just as your nickname is Billy, but your real name is William." "S'not either, it's Billy," came the reply. "Well," I said, "people call you Billy, but your real name is William." "Billy," he muttered. At this point the classroom teacher intervened and said in steely tones, "Your name is William!" Somewhat nonplussed I went ahead with the lesson, letting the children handle the instrument, pluck and bow the strings, then listen to an older child play it. At the end of the period, to review, I again held the instrument up and asked, "What is this instrument?" Came a voice from the back of the room—"It's a William."

I was young—I was confusing *naming* with *understanding: words* with *functions*. This book is not concerned with naming things, except occasionally, but it is concerned with basic skills and concepts—the functional side of music. This is what the Kodály concept is all about.

Shortly after the first appearance of the Kodály Method in this country, I began working with it in spite of the dearth of authentic information on it available in English. Then, it was my good fortune to meet Katinka Daniel, graduate of the Franz Liszt Academy of Music (Budapest) and pupil of Kodály, who became my friend and teacher and who guided me through the next two years of my work. When I felt that I had come to a point where I did not know what to do next, it was Mrs. Daniel who suggested that I go to Hungary and learn firsthand.

This I did in the summer of 1968. I attended the Danube Bend Summer University at Esztergom. At that summer course I saw and heard group after group of Hungarian school children—singing, reading, writing music. I saw music permeating the life of the Hungarian people, in villages and in cities. I saw enough in that three-week summer university course to know I had only scratched the surface. I *had* to return to study the Method in depth.

This I did during the academic year 1970–71 at the Franz Liszt Academy. I learned much in that year—and yet I still find myself wishing I could return to ask a question, to observe again a procedure. The superficial simplicity of the Method is deceptive. There always seems to be something more to learn about it.

As of this writing I have been to Hungary three times and feel sure I shall be returning again, for the Kodály Method is an evolving method. It has changed greatly since its inception almost thirty years ago, and is sure to continue to change as better ways are found to instill in children love of music and knowledge about music.

For many beautifully-taught lessons and many helpful discussions about curriculum and methodology of music in Hungarian schools, I am greatly indebted to Mrs. Anna Hamvas, Mrs. Helga Szabó, Mrs. Emma Serényi, Mrs. Katalin Forrai, Mrs. Marta Nemesszeghy, Mrs. Eszter Mihályi, Miss Klára Nemes, and Mr. Miklos Csik.

To Laszlo Vikar, ethnomusicologist and member of the Hungarian Academy of Sciences, I owe my ability to analyze folk songs. The sessions with him on folk music research were invaluable.

A special debt of thanks must go to Mrs. Zoltán Kodály, who gave freely of her time to help me with the history of the Method, an aspect which has not previously been treated fully in English.

Great teachers are few—Erzsébet Szönyi, Dean of the School of Music Education at the Franz Liszt Academy of Music in Budapest, is surely the most outstanding pedagogue with whom I have ever worked. I am grateful to her not only for the work she did in helping to arrange for my year in Hungary, but also for the many private interviews I had with her, and for the advice she has proffered at various stages during the writing of this book. I am deeply honored that she has chosen to write the foreword.

I am also indebted to Nicholas Geriak, Supervisor in Baltimore County (Maryland), for encouraging me to investigate something new and different in music education. Without the support, moral and financial, of an open-minded school system, the past years of experimentation and study would have been impossible.

In closing, I must thank the kind people who made of Hungary a second home for me—György Czeller and his wife Sarolta—and also my husband, Lee, who encouraged me from the very beginning of this project, who read and discussed this book with me page by page as it was written. Neither the Czellers nor my husband is a musician and yet without them this book surely would not have been written.

part I

The Kodály Method in Hungary

chapter I

The Beginnings of the Method in Hungary and Its International Spread

Music seems to be part of the very fiber of Hungarian life. Hungary, a nation the size of Indiana, with a population of ten million people, has eight hundred adult concert choirs, fifty of the first rank and another one hundred of radio or public performance quality. There are four professional symphony orchestras in Budapest alone and five in country towns, as well as numerous amateur orchestras. A man without a musical education is considered illiterate. Almost all play instruments; almost all sing. Concert halls are full.

The situation was not always so. Early in the 1900s, Zoltán Kodály, the noted Hungarian composer and educator, was appalled at the level of musical literacy he found in students entering the Zeneakademia—the highest music school in Hungary. Not only were these students unable to read and write music fluently, but in addition, they were totally ignorant of their own musical heritage. Since they had grown up in the aftermath of the Austro-Hungarian Empire, a time when only German and Viennese music were considered "good" music by the elite, the only exposure these students had had to the vast wealth of Hungarian folk music was through the distorted and diluted versions played by gypsies in cafés.

Kodály felt deeply that it must be his mission to give back to the people of Hungary their own musical heritage and to raise the level of musical literacy, not only in academy students but also in the population as a whole.

As a first step in this direction he sought to improve teacher training. In his words:

> It is much more important who is the music teacher in Kisvárda than who is the director of the opera house in Budapest . . . for a poor director fails

once, but a poor teacher keeps on failing for 30 years, killing the love of music in 30 batches of children.

Kodály was almost single-handedly responsible for causing the required music in teacher-training programs to be increased from one-half year to three years, to the present five-year teacher's diploma program at the Academy.

However, his interest in music education only began at the teacher-training level. His strong commitment to making music belong to everyone, not just to the educated upper classes, soon led him to become involved in the education of young children, and further, to involve all those around him. His fellow professors at the Academy, his colleagues in the area of folk music collection and analysis, even his more talented pupils, all became involved in his dream of a musically literate nation.

Kodály had been interested in the collection and analysis of Hungarian folk music since the turn of the century. With Béla Bartók he collected some one thousand children's songs which, when analyzed and classified according to mode, scale, and type by Dr. György Kerényi, eventually became the first volume of the massive Corpus Musicae Popularis Hungaricae. This work of collecting, analyzing, classifying, and publishing Hungarian folk music, started by Bartók and Kodály, continues today at the Academy of Sciences in Budapest. At present there are five volumes of the Corpus Musicae, covering the above-mentioned children's songs, holiday and festival songs, courting songs, wedding songs, and laments. Many further volumes are planned.

In view of his great knowledge of and love for the music of the peasants of Hungary, it is not surprising that Kodály chose this music as the vehicle through which to teach children. In doing this, however, he had reasons other than simply his love for it. He felt that as a child naturally learns his mother tongue before foreign languages, he should learn his musical mother tongue—i.e., the folk music of his own country—before other music. He likened the historical development of music from primitive folk song to art music to the development of the child from infant to adult. In addition, he considered the simple short forms, the basically pentatonic scale, and the simplicity of the language all characteristics which would contribute to good pedagogical use of such music with children.

But perhaps most important, he considered that folk music represented a living art. It was not contrived for pedagogical purposes. It already existed and fit well into a systematic scheme for teaching the concepts and skills of music to young children. Kodály insisted upon using only the purest of authentic folk music with children. This specification is still observed today. Although the textbooks used in the Singing

Schools are written by master teachers, before publication they are given to ethnomusicologists at the Academy of Sciences for critical opinion. No spurious example is allowed to remain simply because it fulfills a teaching function. When a better variant of a particular folk song is known, changes in the books are made accordingly.

However, folk music was not to be the only material of the Method. If the step between folk music and art music was to be bridged, then it was necessary that there be good composed music suitable for children to sing. It was in 1923 that Kodály began composing works for children's choirs and studying musical education in the schools in depth.

The first book which might actually be considered as leading toward the Kodály Method as it is known today was a song book, *Énekes ABC*, compiled by György Kerényi and Benjámin Rajeczky, and published by Magyar Kórus, Budapest, in 1938. This was followed in 1940 by a companion text book *Éneklö Iskola* (A Singing School). This text, with its materials taken largely from the folk songs collected by Kodály and Bartók, was aimed not at young children but at the lycée or intermediate grade level. It was used in a number of schools in Hungary, and its pedagogy was tested by, among others, Kodály's friend Irma Bors, a Sister of Charity then teaching in the largest secondary school in Budapest, and also by György Gulyás, the present director of the Academy of Music at Debrécen, who was then teaching at a private resident school in the country, where music for the first time was taught daily as a core subject in the curriculum.

The next text in the Method, and the first attempt at a text for young children, was *Iskolai Énekegyüjtemény* (A School Collection of Songs) by Kerényi and Kodály, published in Budapest in 1943. This text contained one volume for ages six to ten and a second volume for ages eleven to fourteen. The material in them ranged from easy Hungarian children's songs to fairly difficult songs with evidence of foreign influence. It is to accompany these that Kodály composed his volume *333 Exercises*.

These books are of great interest to anyone studying the evolution of the Method, since they begin with a song built entirely on one pitch and then progress to songs built on the major second. It took very little time for teachers using these books to realize that a song built on a single tone was all but impossible for young children to sing in tune, and that even the major second as a starting point presented difficulties.

It was for this reason that when, at the urging of Kodály, Jenö Adám wrote his *Módszéres Énektanitás* (Systematic Singing Teaching), Turul, Budapest, 1944, he began melodic training with the minor third, the most natural interval for young children to sing in tune. Even in this Adám book the speed with which the teacher was expected to move from one concept or skill to the next was found to be unrealistically fast, and is far removed from the slow systematic pace of the eight graded books, *Enek Zene,* by Márta Nemesszeghy (grades one–five) and Helga Szabó (grades six–eight) now used in the Hungarian Singing Schools.

It is unfortunate that many American adaptations of the Kodály Method have copied almost verbatim this early Adám text, rather than using the excellent current Nemesszeghy ones as their guide.

The next volume of particular interest after the Adám book was one specifically aimed at *sol-fa* teaching as a preparation for instrumental study, *Introductory Course in Music* by Vera Irsai, Cserépfalir, Budapest, 1947. In this the principles of deriving musical learning from folk song material were clearly defined.

Perhaps the most complete volumes to appear in the Method are the *sol-fa* books of Kodály's pupil Erzsébet Szönyi, who at present is professor of music at the Franz Liszt Academy of Music in Budapest and a composer of stature in her own right. These books, *A Zenei Írás-Olvasás Módzsertana,* Volumes I, II, and III (Methods of Sight-Reading and Notation), Zeneműkiadó, Budapest, 1953, combine all the elements of what has come to be known as the Kodály Method: the tonic *sol-fa* system, the Curwen hand signs, the shifting *do* with key change, and the reliance on the best of folk and composed song material for teaching purposes. These books are used today in Hungary in the Special Music Preparatory Schools, the Conservatories, and the Academy of Music.

However, books alone do not make a system of education. It was in the schools and in the hands of the teachers that the Method truly evolved and is still evolving, for the Kodály Method is a living method, not a static one. As better ways are found, they are incorporated.

Together with his good friend Márta Nemesszeghy, Kodály persuaded the Ministry of Education to allow an experiment in music education in the town of his birth, Kecskemét. Starting with just one class, using the Kodály materials and method, and having music every day, Márta Nemesszeghy achieved such success that where there was one Singing Primary School in Hungary in 1950, there are now more than 130. More are planned as enough trained teachers become available.

One reason Kodály and Márta Nemesszeghy were able to convince the Ministry of Education to continue and even to expand the Singing Primary Schools was an unusual side effect of such music instruction on the learning in other subject areas. An unexpected result of daily music instruction via the Kodály Method was a marked improvement of achievement in other academic areas. This was particularly true of mathematics, seeming to bear out Thorndike's theory that disciplines having common elements are mutually affected by changes in either. The difference in achievement between the experimental music groups and the matching control groups was enough to be statistically significant, and has been reported by Gabor Friss in the book *Musical Education in Hungary,* Corvina Press, Budapest, 1966, as well as by psychologist Klara Kokas at the 1964 meeting of the International Society for Music Education (I.S.M.E.) in Budapest. Experimentation in this aspect of the Method is still continuing.

But it was not the transfer effect that attracted musicians and educators to Hungary. It was the quality of the music education itself. Music educators came to Hungary from all over the world to study the phenomenal results of the Singing Primary Schools.

The Kodály Method is being practiced today in schools of Eastern and Western Europe, Japan, Australia, North and South America, and Iceland. Adaptations and expositions of the Method have been published in Estonian, Polish, Swedish, Japanese, French, German, Latvian, Spanish, Russian, and, of course, English.

International awareness of the Hungarian music education system perhaps began with the I.S.M.E. Conferences in Vienna in 1958 and in Tokyo in 1963, where reports on the Method were presented, and the 1964 Conference in Budapest, where Zoltán Kodály gave an address and was elected honorary president. It was the latter conference that seemed to cause the beginnings of widespread international interest, since those attending it could see the results of the system firsthand.

The first known export of the Method was to Estonia, U.S.S.R., in the capital city of Tallinn, where the Estonian educator Heino Kaljuste brought about the publication of the Hungarian singing school textbooks in Estonian. The Estonian language, like Hungarian, is of Finno-Ugrian origin, although the two languages have few words in common today. However, it was probably the commonality of ancient culture that made the Hungarian books and songs so appropriate to Estonia. When the work of the first experimental school became public knowledge, the Method spread rapidly and is practiced today in every Estonian school and in a number of schools in neighboring Latvia.

In Leningrad, Academician Pavel Filipovitch Weiss wrote a dissertation on the Method for his academic degree of candidature, referring to both the Estonian and the Hungarian examples. He later visited Hungary and addressed a conference on music education at Györ on the spread of the concept of Kodály in the Soviet Union, where today it is widely accepted.

The International Folk Music Council (I.F.M.C.), of which Kodály was president, met in Budapest in 1964. During this meeting Kodály arranged a visit for the participants to the singing primary school in Kecskemét. This visit resulted in the profound interest of two of the conference participants, Dr. Jacques Chailley of the Sorbonne University in France and Dr. Alexander Ringer of the University of Illinois. Dr.

Chailley was instrumental in arranging for Jacquotte Ribière-Raverlat to spend an academic year in Hungary in 1965–66—a year which resulted in the first French language exposition of the Method: L'Education Musicale dans Hongrie. Twice since that conference Dr. Ringer has taken a group of ten young Americans to Hungary to study the method firsthand.

The Method's spread to Canada probably had its inception with the visit of Erzsébet Szönyi in 1965 to the French-speaking territories, where she presented a series of lectures on Hungarian music education. There was interest in these from the English-speaking areas as well; today there are regular summer courses on the Kodály Method all over Canada, and the system is used in the schools of Montreal, Toronto, and Halifax. Textbooks for children have been published in French, and the method is being taught in a number of teacher-training institutions.

The ideas of Kodály were first exposed in the United States through the writings of Mary Helen Richards, whose Theshold to Music books and charts, written after a brief visit to Hungary, if somewhat limited in scope and uncertain in sequence, nevertheless were responsible to a large extent for the present widespread popularity of the Method in the United States. In 1966 Kodály and Erzsébet Szönyi participated in the I.S.M.E. Conference at Interlochen, Michigan, and went on to Stanford University in August to attend a symposium on the Method. At this symposium Mrs. Richards gave demonstrations with children, and both Kodály and Erzsébet Szönyi presented lectures. It was during the Stanford symposium that Denise Bacon became interested in the Method —an interest that led her to become the first American to spend an academic year in Hungary, studying the Method firsthand in 1968–69. This culminated in the Founding of the American Kodály Institute at Wellesley, Massachusetts, for the dissemination of accurate knowledge about the Method and for teacher training in the Method.

In South America, too, the ideas of Kodály are known. In Argentina, Ladislaus Domonko worked with the Method, first using Hungarian song materials and later finding suitable Argentine folk songs for the skill and concept sequence. He reported on this work in the book Metodo Kodály in 1969. In 1970 Laszló Ördög, Supervisor of Music for the Budapest schools, spent a year teaching in Chile and reported that use of the Method was widespread in both Chile and Peru.

The existence of the Kodály Method in Japan is largely due to the efforts of one musician and teacher, Hani Kyoto, who spent some years in Hungary studying before returning to Tokyo to found the Japanese Kodály Institute. This institute has trained numerous teachers in the Method and has published books in the Method for the first four grades, using Japanese folk song materials. There proved to be a number of unexpected similarities in rhythms and scales between Hungarian and Japanese folk music, particularly early childhood music.

The Method traveled to Czechoslovakia with Alois Slozik, director of the music school at Jesenik. Since his first contact with the Method at the Esztergom Summer University in 1967, Czech teachers have come to study at this Summer Kodály course in Esztergom each year.

The Summer University Course on Kodály at Esztergom has at this writing trained several thousand people from thirty-one countries. Recently Mrs. Zoltan Kodály organized a Summer Kodály Seminar at Kesckemét, Kodály's birthplace and the home of the first public singing school in Hungary. This summer course is closely related to the American Kodály Institute at Wellesley and, like the Esztergom Summer University course, is training large numbers of teachers from many countries.

As early as 1958 there was interest in the Kodály Method in Germany, fostered by Professor Egon Kraus, then the Secretary-General of I.S.M.E. By 1965 the Method was actively in use in a number of German schools, and in 1971 the third Kodály Institute was founded, this time in Germany.

The Method traveled to Belgium as a result of a cultural exchange program in which one of the stated purposes was to incorporate the Hungarian method into Belgian schools.

Large groups of teachers from Denmark, Iceland, Finland, and Switzerland have come to Hungary to visit the schools and to observe the Method. These visits have resulted in invitations to Hungarian teachers to present teacher-training courses in these countries. A Danish adaptation of the Method by Klara Fredborg is now in use in a number of schools.

In England, one of the first countries to be aware of the Kodály pedagogical compositions, the Hungarian system is being practiced in a number of schools and universities. Perhaps because of the availability of English language translations by Percy Young and by Geoffrey Russell-Smith, the Method is well known in Australia as well.

In all these languages, in all these adaptations and approaches to the Method, one basic principle is clear: Kodály's conception of music as a basic academic subject equal in importance to language, mathematics, and the social sciences. Although he believed deeply in the emotional values of music, Kodály nevertheless felt it imperative that love of music be supported by knowledge about music. He felt that one could not exist intelligently without the other. In his own words:

Music is a manifestation of the human spirit, similar to language. Its greatest practitioners have conveyed to mankind things not possible to say in any other language. If we do not want these things to remain dead treasures, we must do our utmost to make the greatest possible number of people understand their idiom.

Preface

A Zenei Írás-Olvasás Módszertana

1953

It is unlikely that Kodály ever thought of what was taking place in the Singing Schools of Hungary as the "Kodály Method." He knew too well the numbers of musicians, teachers, and ethnomusicologists involved in its creation and ongoing development to take such credit for himself. It remained for foreigners visiting Hungary to give Kodály's name to what they saw. And yet he was the driving force behind what happened in the schools of Hungary. Almost until the day of his death he was visiting schools, talking with teachers, conferring on curriculum, and, in passing, jotting down a musical phrase to be sung at sight by a child here or there.

While the Method came from the joint efforts of many people, it was without doubt Kodály's vision that gave it breath. All who worked with him speak of him still as a continuing influence in their lives and work. The Kodály Method has become to Hungarians and to many others a living monument to the man who inspired it.

chapter 2

The Method: Its Sequence, Tools, and Materials

Zoltan Kodály wished to see a unified system of music education evolve in Hungary, capable of leading children towards love of and knowledge about music from earliest nursery school years to adulthood. To this end he devoted a significant part of his creative life. The method which emerged under his direction and which is the official music curriculum of schools in Hungary is based on singing, on the study of good musical material, folk and composed, and on the method of relative solmization. Its objectives are twofold: to aid in the well-balanced social and artistic development of the child, and to produce the musically literate adult—literate in the fullest sense of being able to look at a musical score and think sound, to read and write music as easily as words. Although interested in the training of professional musicians, Kodály's first concern was the musically literate amateur. He wished to see an education system that could produce a people to whom music was not a way to make a living but a way of life.

What Is the Sequence of the Method?

The sequence which was developed in Hungary, after much experimentation, is a child-developmental one rather than one based on subject logic. In a subject-logic approach there is no relationship between the order of presentation and the order in which children learn easily. The subject matter is simply organized in a fashion that seems reasonable in terms of content.

Most music teachers are familiar with the subject-logic approach to music teaching. Rhythmically, it begins with the whole note and then proceeds to halves and quarters—a mathematically reasonable progression, but a very difficult one for the beginning student who has not yet been taught even to feel the basic beat. Melodically, the diatonic major scale is generally considered the subject-logic starting point for teaching music. Yet the average young child cannot accurately sing the diatonic major scale. According to research, he is able to sing a range of only five or six tones and cannot produce half-steps in tune.[1,2] To use a subject-logic approach in teaching music to the young child is to expect him to intellectualize about something that does not in reality exist in his own experiences.

What Is Meant by a "Child-Developmental" Approach as Used in the Kodály Method?

The child-developmental approach to sequence within a subject requires the arrangement of the subject matter into patterns that follow normal child abilities at various stages of growth.

In terms of rhythm, moving rhythms are more child-related than sustained ones. The quarter note is the child's walking pace, the eighth note, his running. These are the rhythms of the child's day-to-day living. His singing games are largely made up of quarter- and eighth-note patterns in duple meter. They are a more reasonable starting place for teaching rhythm concepts to children than whole notes.

Melodically, the first tones sung by young children are the minor third. They are the tones his mother uses to call him to dinner:

Tom - my!

They are the tones of many of his own sing-song chants:

I   am   big - ger   than   you   are

If we consider this minor third to be *so-mi,* the next tone the young child can usually sing in tune is the *la* above. The common pattern in Hungarian children's chants is the *la* on a weak beat following *so:*

[1] Orpha K. Duell and Richard C. Anderson, "Pitch Discrimination Among Primary School Children," *Journal of Educational Psychology,* 58, No. 6 (1957), 315–18.

[2] Rosamund Shuter, *The Psychology of Musical Ability* (London: Methuen and Co., Ltd., 1968).

ha   én   ci - ca   vol - nék,
        └─┘
      maj. 2nd

In most American three-note chants and songs the *la* is approached from *mi*, forming a rising fourth on a weak beat:

John - ny   is   a   sis - sy!
            └──┘
          perfect 4th

Interestingly enough, up to this point children seem to develop in the same musical pattern the world over. Young children's games and chants based on these two or three notes are found from the U.S.A. to Hungary to Japan. The order in which these notes occur may differ, but the minor third and the major second above it are the universal musical vocabulary of young children.

Obviously, then, a developmental approach to the teaching of vocal music would use simple duple-meter rhythms and these three notes as its starting point.

There are other characteristics of the musical development of young children, which must play a part in determining any developmental sequence.

1. The range of young children's voices is limited—usually not more than five or six tones, and these of whole steps or larger intervals. Half steps are difficult for the young child to sing in tune.

2. Descending tones are easier, with the exception of the previously-mentioned fourth, for children to learn and reproduce accurately than ascending ones. This indicates that the initial lesson on new tonal patterns should be approached through songs in which the interval occurs in a descending melody line.

3. Skips are easier for the young child to sing in tune than steps: G to E is easier than G to F.

4. In terms of range, one study has shown that left to his own devices the young child will most often pitch the upper note of the minor third around F♯. Thus the keys of D, E♭, and E would seem to be indicated for pitching teacher-initiated rote songs.

Most of these findings were made, curiously enough, almost simultaneously in Hungary by the people then working on the Kodály Method, in Switzerland where the Willems method, still in use at present, was being developed, and in the U.S.A. by a research team in California.[3] Even the Orff Institute in Austria, with its instrumental rather than vocal orientation, seems to have discovered these same basic developmental concepts.

Recognizing these principles as factors in the melodic development of children, Kodály felt that the pentaton—the five-tone scale—was the ideal vehicle for teaching children musical skills. The pentaton is one of the basic scales of folk music in Hungary and in most of the world, although the pentaton of Hungarian music tends to be minor in character, or *la*-centered, while the usual American pentatonic song is major, or *do*-centered.*

The melodic sequence that gradually evolved in Hungary was:

1. The minor third (*so-mi*),
2. *la* and its intervals with *so* and *mi*,
3. *do*, the "home tone" in major modes, and the intervals it forms with *so*, *mi*, and *la*,
4. *re*, the last remaining tone of the pentaton.

After these five tones the octaves low *la*, low *so*, and high *do* are taught, and, last, the half steps *fa* and *ti*, to complete the diatonic major and minor scales.

The Tools of the Method

The first of the tools chosen for use in the Kodály Method was the movable-*do* system of solmization originated by Guido d'Arezzo in the eleventh century. In this system the home tone or tonal center of a song is *do* in the major and *la* in the minor modes, whatever the key may be. The advantages of this for teaching vocal sight-reading should be obvious. The basic tune of the minor third *so-mi* is the same in any key. Thus when a child knows only these two notes he can already read them in any placement on the staff. As his sight-singing vocabulary increases to the five tones of the pentaton, he can read far more than only three lines and two spaces.

For teaching rhythm Kodály and the teachers working with him chose

---

3 Gladys Moorhead and Dònald Pond, *Music of Young Children,* Vols. 1–4 (Santa Barbara, Calif.: Pillsbury Foundation for Advanced Music Education, 1941–1951).

* This seeming difference in scales is discussed in more detail in Chapter 10.

a syllable system similar to that used in French solfege—i.e., the quarter note is "ta" and the eighth note is "ti."

Example:

These syllables are not names but expressions of duration. They are voiced, never written as words. Their written representation is stem notation. With duration syllables it is possible for children to chant a pattern correctly in rhythm, which would be impossible if they used note value names. The words "quar-ter note" contain three separate sounds, although the quarter note has only one sound on one beat. A pattern read, "quarter note, quarter note, eighth note, eighth note, quarter note," if notated according to heard sounds of each syllable, would look like this:

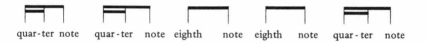

This is not to say that a child should not be able to identify and name quarter notes and eighth notes. Once he firmly understands their duration he should also learn their correct terms. However, for purposes of rhythm *reading* he needs rhythm syllables which express their *duration*.

Basically, the rhythm duration syllables used in the Method are

Rests are taught as beats of silence.

Only the note stems are used initially for rhythm reading. That is, quarter notes are shown as | |, eighth notes as ⌐ ⌐. The body of the note is not necessary to rhythm reading except for half notes and whole notes (♩ o). In all other cases the rhythm is determined by the note stems.

A third tool of the Method is the use of hand signs, which originated with John Curwen in 1870. These have been incorporated, with only minor changes, to reinforce intervallic feeling. They present a visualization in space of the high-low relationship among the notes being sung. For the pentaton the hand signs are

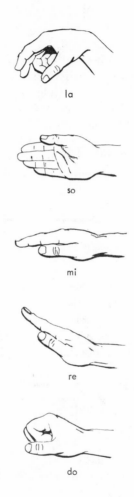

la

so

mi

re

do

The hand signs for the half steps *ti-do* and *fa-mi,* taught later, are

ti which points up to *do:*

do

ti

fa which points down to *mi:*

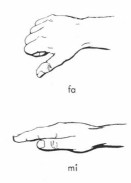

fa

mi

thus emphasizing the smallness of these half steps. The hand signs are shown here as the person making them with his right hand sees them. The signs are made in front of the body, with the *do* sign occurring at about waist level, the *la* at about eye level. The distance between the hand signs should reflect, to some extent, the size of the interval being sung and shown. Thus, *so-mi,* a minor third, should be shown as a larger movement in space than *so-la* or *do-re,* major seconds. Octaves are shown by the same sign but in the correct high or low relationship to the rest of the scale. Notes above high *do* are shown in writing by a prime (or comma) above the syllable: *la';* notes below low *do,* by a prime (or comma) below: *la,*.

In writing, only the first letter of the *sol-fa* scale step is used, not the whole word. Thus, *do* becomes *d*, *re* becomes *r*, etc. This, combined with stem notation, provides a sort of musical shorthand which makes writing music without staff paper both easy and fast.

Example:

```
   d    d    s    s    l    l    s
 twin-kle twin-kle lit-tle  star
```

Such notation can easily be converted to staff notation later from this shorthand.

The Materials of the Method

Nothing about this sequence or these tools is unique to the Kodály Method. Singly, each has been tried before, and even in combinations they may be found in some methods used many years ago in the U.S. and Europe.

However, the one area in which the Kodály approach differs from its predecessors and achieves what none of the others has, is in the selection of materials. Kodály insisted that the materials used for teaching music to young children could come from only three sources:

1. Authentic children's games and nursery songs,
2. Authentic folk music,
3. Good composed music, i.e., music written by recognized composers.

Kodály felt that the simple, expressive forms of nursery songs and folk music were more suitable for children because they were living music, not fabricated or contrived for pedagogical purposes. The language of folk music tends to be simple, drawn from speech patterns familiar to children even before they enter school.

In addition, Kodály felt there was a close relationship between the music of the people and the music of great composers. He believed that a love for the masterworks could be cultivated through a knowledge of and a love for one's own folk music.

To implement the use of good music in the schools, Kodály collected great numbers of children's songs and folk songs. Working with Kerenyi and Rajeczky, Kodály published six massive volumes of Hungarian folk music, the first of which contains more than 1,000 children's songs.

Most of the teaching material in the school books of Hungary today is still chosen from the material collected by Kodály and his associates, of whom fellow composer Béla Bartók was one. Kodály's work of collection and analysis is still being carried on today by ethnomusicologists at the Folk Music Institute in Budapest.

To implement the third source of materials—that of good composed music—Kodály himself wrote much music for children: four volumes of pentatonic music, numerous volumes of two- and three-part exercises, the *Bicinia Hungarica* (two- and three-part compositions based on folk music), and many children's choruses. Bartók, too, wrote for children: the *Mikrokosmos* for piano students, and a number of songs for children's choruses. Among Kodály's composition pupils, Erzsébet Szönyi, the present Dean of the Franz Liszt Academy of Music, has composed many works for children.

But the "good composed music" taught to Hungarian children is not all Kodály and Bartók. In the elementary years the children also sing works ranging from Monteverdi, Bach, and Handel, through Mozart and Haydn, to Beethoven, Brahms, and Schumann, and many other composers of the Baroque, Classical, and Romantic periods. In seventh and eighth grades the children also sing and study the works of twentieth-century foreign composers.

Conclusion

The Kodály Method is an approach to teaching the skills of music literacy to young children. Its sequence is a child-developmental one, based on the normal musical progression of children from the minor third, through the notes of the pentaton, to the full scales of the major and minor modes.

The tools used to implement this sequence are the movable-*do* system of solmization, rhythm-duration syllables, and the Curwen hand signs.

The materials of the Method are authentic children's songs and folk song material, and the music of great composers.

It is probably this last—the insistence on authentic folk music and good composed music—that makes the Kodály Method unique. Music literacy is of little value if at the same time the child is not given the skills for musical discrimination. Without these he has no basis for selection. The child who has grown up in an environment of good music will perhaps be more likely to support and participate in musical organizations. Such has been the experience in Hungary, where the Method has produced musically literate amateurs—as is its aim—not just professionals. As an example, factory workers in Hungary form local symphony orchestras and concert choirs rather than bowling teams for their own recreation.

chapter 3

The Structure of Public Education

in Hungary and the Place of Music

in That Structure

In order to understand better the place of music education in Hungary, one needs to understand the organization of the school system as a whole.

The earliest available public education, the nursery school, is an integral part of Hungarian public education, directed by the Ministry of Education. Nursery school education has existed in Hungary for many years. The first nursery school was established in 1828, and as early as 1891 there was a parliamentary law enacted providing for the education of preschool children. Since 1945 the development of the nursery school-kindergarten program has greatly accelerated. Today there are more than 3200 nursery schools in Hungary. Since schooling before age six is voluntary rather than compulsory, the attendance in cities, where, usually, both parents work, is considerably higher than in rural districts, where the mother is more likely to stay at home with young children.

Nursery schools are of three basic types, varying with the needs of the communities in which they operate. There are nursery schools for half-day sesssions only, which do not offer meals to children; there are nursery schools that provide full-day care for the children of working parents and offer three meals a day; and there are actual resident nursery schools, offering day and night care with full board, six days a week. The greatest number of nursery schools belong to the second category, those offering day care with meals.

In general, nursery schools are open year-round, without the usual school holidays, since child care is a necessity for working parents, although there are some which follow the normal school calendar year and some which operate on full-day sessions only in the summer to accommodate the needs of agricultural communities.

There are no fees for the schooling, but a small charge, based on the family's income, is made for meals.

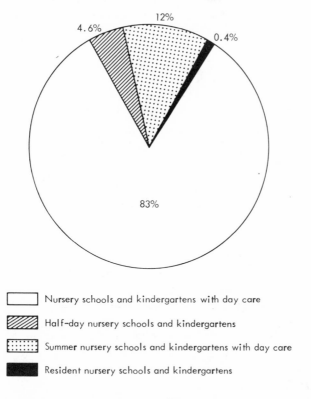

Nursery schools and kindergartens with day care

Half-day nursery schools and kindergartens

Summer nursery schools and kindergartens with day care

Resident nursery schools and kindergartens

Figure 1. **The Division of Nursery Schools and Kindergartens According to Their Types**

Within the schools the children are grouped by age into classes of twenty-two to twenty-five. The staff of such a school includes teachers specifically trained for nursery schools, as well as aides, cafeteria help, and custodians. A complete staff is necessary since nursery schools are housed in buildings completely removed from the primary schools, rather than being included in the local elementary school building as most American kindergartens are.

The stated aim of such schools is to:

lay the basis of the education and bringing up of the children in order to make them healthy and physically trained, patriotic, conscientious, well-disciplined, and cultured people.[1]

[1] Ernö Buti, *Public Education in the Hungarian People's Republic* (Budapest: Ministry of Public Education, 1966), p. 67.

The curriculum through which to achieve this aim has been spelled out in a handbook for teachers. Play, work, and instruction are given as the means to education of the preschool child, and specific content is included in five areas of preschool education: 1) physical education, 2) mother tongue and environment, 3) elements of quantity, form, and space, 4) art, and 5) music. Although listed last, music is considered to be of equal importance with the other four areas of instruction. A detailed description of the place of music in the nursery school curriculum is given in Chapter 4.

In Hungary compulsory education begins with the eight-year General Primary School (Általános Iskola) for children ages six to fourteen. These schools have a state-defined compulsory curriculum and state-approved and published textbooks in all subjects.

The eight grades of the General Primary School must be completed satisfactorily by the child in a maximum of ten years. Any child failing to achieve this must continue school attendance for two more years in a special "continuation" or special training school which usually provides agricultural or industrial training.

The school year is ten months, September to June, and class periods, even in the early grades, are forty-five minutes for each subject. Because of the extreme shortage of facilities, most schools operate on double sessions, the morning shift beginning at 8 A.M. and the afternoon shift not ending until 6 P.M. or, in some cases, 7 P.M. Both teachers and pupils alternate shifts, mornings one week, afternoons the next, so as to avoid hardship on any one group.

Children in the lower grades, one to four, are generally taught in self-contained classrooms, while some departmentalization is practiced with the upper-grade children (grades five to eight).

The academic curriculum in the General Primary School is not unlike the elementary school curriculum of many schools in the U.S. Reading, writing, and mathematics are considered of prime importance, along with the building of social attitudes. There are, of course, some obvious differences in curriculum. The study of Russian is compulsory, and other languages are available as electives, beginning in the fourth grade.

Music in the General Primary School is taught for two forty-five-minute periods a week, and, in addition, all General Primary Schools have two required hours a week of choir for children in grades five to eight. In most of these schools the grade teacher is responsible for music instruction in the lower grades, and the music specialist in the upper grades. In order to ensure that the teachers in the lower grades are competent to handle music, there are stringent entrance requirements in music at the teacher-training institutes, and there is further concentrated music instruction during the teacher-training period. Even so, the music

Subject	Number of Lessons in the							
	Grade of General Classes							
	1st	2nd	3rd	4th	5th	6th	7th	8th
1. Hungarian language and literature	—	—	—	—	6	5	5	5
2. Reading	—	5	4	4	—	—	—	—
3. Writing	10	2	2	2	—	—	—	—
4. Composition	—	—	2	2	—	—	—	—
5. Grammar and spelling	—	3	3	3	—	—	—	—
6. Knowledge of environment	1	2	2	2	—	—	—	—
7. Russian	—	—	—	—	3	3	3	3
8. History	—	—	—	—	2	2	2	2
9. Geography	—	—	—	—	2	2	2	2
10. Mathematics, geometry	5	6	6	6	5	5	4	4
11. Physics	—	—	—	—	—	2	2	2
12. Chemistry	—	—	—	—	—	—	2	2
13. Living world	—	—	—	—	2	2	2	2
14. Practical exercises	1	1	2	2	2	2	2	2
15. Drawing	—	1	1	2	2	2	2	2
16. Singing, music	1	2	2	2	2	2	2	2
17. Physical training	2	2	2	2	2	2	2	2
18. Choir-singing	—	—	—	—	2	2	2	2

Chart 1. Hours per Week in Various Subject Areas for Grades 1 to 8 in the General Primary School

			Number of Lessons in the					
Subject	1st	2nd	3rd	4th	5th	6th	7th	8th
				Grade of Singing-Music Classes				
1. Hungarian language and literature	—	—	—	—	6	5	5	5
2. Reading	—	5	4	4	—	—	—	—
3. Writing	10	2	2	2	—	—	—	—
4. Composition	—	—	2	2	—	—	—	—
5. Grammar and spelling	—	3	3	3	—	—	—	—
6. Knowledge of environment	1	2	2	2	—	—	—	—
7. Russian	—	—	—	—	3	3	3	3
8. History	—	—	—	—	2	2	2	2
9. Geography	—	—	—	—	2	2	2	2
10. Mathematics, geometry	5	6	6	6	5	5	4	4
11. Physics	—	—	—	—	—	2	2	2
12. Chemistry,	—	—	—	—	—	—	2	2
13. Living world	—	—	—	—	2	2	2	2
14. Practical exercises	1	1	2	2	2	2	2	2
15. Drawing	—	1	1	2	2	2	2	2
16. Singing, music	5	6	6	6	4	4	4	4
17. Physical training	2	2	2	2	2	2	2	2
18. Choir-singing	—	—	—	—	2	2	2	2

Chart 2. Hours per Week in Various Subject Areas for Grades 1 to 8 in the Singing Primary School

instruction in the lower grades of the General Primary Schools is not always adequate. It is at its best in cities where there are enough trained music teachers to be able to take the program out of the hands of the classroom teachers.

In addition to the General Primary Schools there are also Singing Primary Schools, encompassing grades one through eight, in which music is given equal importance in the curriculum with reading, writing, and mathematics. Music in these schools is considered to be a basic subject and, accordingly, its time allotment is equal to that of mathematics or reading: an hour a day, six days a week, for a total of as many as *198* hours a year.

The music teachers in these schools are highly trained musicians, most of them graduates of the teacher-training program of the Franz Liszt Academy of Music in Budapest or of one of its six affiliate teacher-training institutes. An average Singing Primary School might have four or more such teachers on its staff. Each teacher is responsible for only three or four different classes.

The children who attend these schools are selected. Although such selection is contrary to the philosophy of Kodály, who envisioned the Singing Primary School as the path to universal music literacy, it became necessary simply because of the great numbers of applicants, the limited amount of space, and the difficulties in finding enough qualified teachers.

There are at present more than 130 Singing Primary Schools in Hungary, but this is out of a total of 6200 primary schools. Each spring parents are invited to bring their five- and six-year-olds to apply for admission to the Singing Primary Schools. Where space for thirty children may exist, often one hundred or more apply. The ever-increasing number of applicants has made it necessary to devise some process for selection. This process varies somewhat from school to school, but generally, the child is asked to sing a simple nursery song, to repeat an easy four-beat rhythm after the teacher, and to sing, in imitation of the teacher, a melodic phrase of small range. The music teachers in the school act as a committee in making the final selections.

Obviously, even such simple tests could result in the selection of only those children with strong music potential. However, because of Kodály's conviction that music must not be for the elite but for everyone, a special effort is made to choose a certain number of children from those who do not perform well in the entrance examination. There is no specific number who must come from this category, but it is the practice of all Singing Primary Schools to take some students who seem musically less able, who perhaps cannot match pitch or repeat a rhythm correctly. It is felt that in this way the spirit, if not the letter, of Kodály's intentions is honored. As more teachers become available, new Singing Primary

Schools open, but it will be many years before the supply of teachers trained in the Method equals the demand.

The Singing Primary School is usually housed in the same building with a General Primary School. In the one building there may be three classes at each grade level, two general classes and one singing class. The music teachers for the two schools are not usually the same since a Singing Primary School music teacher may have responsibility for only three or four classes. This is not as light a schedule as it may seem, since these classes meet every day and the necessary after-hours planning involved is extensive.

For both the General Primary School child and the Singing Primary School child more music training is available after school hours in the Special Music Preparatory School. In this school children take a general musicianship course in sol-fa, music reading and writing, and ear training. Such preparation is required before any child is allowed to study an instrument. The child in the Singing Primary School receives much of this instruction as a part of his daily music lesson, but the General Primary School child must take the work during the out-of-school hours. This does not pose the hardship it might seem, since the school day is short and there are preparatory schools convenient to every geographical area.

No one from either the Singing Primary or the General Primary School may begin the study of instrumental music until he has reached a specified level of musicianship, including the ability to read music vocally. This insistence on sight-singing is made in order to ensure that when the instrumental lessons are begun, the association will always be from symbol or note to sound, rather than from symbol to key or button on an instrument. Instrumental teachers may then concentrate on teaching the skills associated with the playing of the instruments. Although there is no rigid rule as to when a child may begin to study an instrument, the general practice is to begin after two years in the Singing Primary School or after one year of extracurricular musicianship instruction for the General Primary School child.

Instrumental lessons are given in special centers, geographically located so as to be available to all children in an area. Sometimes they are housed in the Singing Primary Schools, but more often they occupy separate buildings. All instrumental instruction is considered extracurricular and is done during the half-day the student is not attending regular classes. Each student receives two half-hour private lessons a week. One school may have twelve or more full-time instrumental teachers. There is no class or group instrumental instruction as we know it in the U.S.

Although a charge is made for instrumental lessons, it is kept small enough so that any family can afford it. If the student shows promise, the fee is dropped altogether after the first year.

Upon completion of the eight grades of either the Singing Primary or the General Primary School with supplementary music in the preparatory school and instrumental lessons, the student is in the position of choosing among the three basic types of secondary school which exist in Hungary. There are General Secondary Schools, which provide a continuation of the broad-based education of the general primaries; Vocational Secondary Schools, which train skilled workers in the areas of industry, agriculture, commerce, transport, communications, and hygiene; and Special Secondary Schools of Fine Arts, among which are the Special Music Secondary Schools. It is the first and last of these three types of secondary schools which are of interest here, for both offer broad musical education.

It is to the General Secondary School that the largest number of continuing students go. While many of these schools offer only a general college preparatory program—history, political ideology, mathematics, science, geography, music, art, physical education, and two foreign languages (one of which must be Russian)—others offer intensified study in specific areas such as foreign language, mathematics, natural science, music, or art. A secondary school offering intensified study in one of these fields would be identified, for example, as a "General Secondary School with Emphasis in Mathematics." Students interested in a specific area of study may apply to a secondary school that emphasizes that subject area.

The General Secondary School with Emphasis in Music is a continuation of the Singing Primary School program. Its stated purpose, like that of the Singing Primary School, is the musical education of nonprofessionals. It is not intended as precareer training in music, but as a means of producing literate amateurs and educated concert audiences. Students may enter the General Secondary School with Emphasis in Music from either the Singing Primary or the General Primary School. In the secondary school with music emphasis they receive full academic work to prepare them for admission to a university or other advanced study, in addition to a rich musical program.

There are a number of schools of this type, but two well-known ones are the one at Kecskemét and the one at Székesfehervar. The former, directed by Márta Nemesszeghy, was the first such school and is the one on which all later ones have been patterned.

Young people who wish to pursue musical careers generally attend the third type of secondary school, the Secondary School of Fine Arts. Those relating specifically to music are referred to as "Conservatories" in Hungary; there are six of these, located in Debrecen, Györ, Miskolc, Pécs, Széged, and Budapest. They draw their students from all over the country. As might be expected, most of their students do not come from a Singing Primary School background but, rather, from the General

Subject	General Secondary Schools				General Secondary Schools with Emphasis in Music			
	1st	2nd	3rd	4th	1st	2nd	3rd	4th
		Grade				Grade		
Hungarian language	2	1	1	1	2	1	1	1
Hungarian literature	2	3	3	3	2	3	3	3
History	2	3	3	3	2	3	3	3
Fundamentals of our ideology	—	—	—	3	—	—	—	3
First foreign language	3	3	3	3	3	3	3	3
Second foreign language	2	2	2	2	2	2	2	2
Mathematics	4	4	4	4	4	4	4	4
Mathematical practice	—	—	—	—	—	—	—	—
Physics	—	2	4	4	—	2	4	4
Chemistry	2	2	2	—	2	2	2	—
Biology	2	2	2/0	2	2	2	2/0	2
Psychology	—	—	0/2	—	—	—	0/2	—
Geography	2	2	2	—	2	2	2	—
Drawing, analysis of works of art	2	—	—	1	2	—	—	1
Music—singing	2	1	—	—	5	4	3	3
Physical training	2	2	2	2	2	2	2	2
Practical exercises	5	5	5	5	2	2	2	2
Grade-masters lesson	1	1	1	1	1	1	1	1
Total of weekly lessons	33	33	34	34	33	33	34	34

Chart 3. Comparison of Hours per Week in Various Subject Areas for Grades 1 to 4 in the General Secondary School and the General Secondary School with Emphasis in Music

Primary Schools with after-hours preparatory music school and instrumental study. Performance is emphasized at these schools.

Pupils who wish to enter one of these schools must pass an examination which calls for a high level of instrumental proficiency, melodic dictation, sight-singing in *sol-fa,* aural intervallic identification, and the answering of questions on music theory.

The school day for pupils who are admitted to the conservatory is a long one. Morning hours are spent taking the academic subjects required for university admission. These are taken in a nearby General Secondary School. Musical study, instrument, *sol-fa*, theory, harmony, history of music, ethnomusicology, chamber music, and choir are taken during the afternoons. It is not uncommon for a student's day to begin at 8 A.M. and to end at 7 P.M. However, practice time and homework preparation times are scheduled within the school day.

At the end of the four-year program the student is required to take the same final academic examinations as the secondary school pupil who has not taken the special conservatory work in music. The secondary school certificate he receives upon passing these examinations makes him eligible for university study in any academic area, not simply in music. Some students do elect at this point in their training to enter other fields professionally.

For the student who wishes to continue in music the next step is the entrance examination to the five-year university-level Academy of Music in Budapest. This examination is extremely difficult, encompassing both theoretical and performance abilities. Not every applicant passes it. Those who fail may take a fifth year of study at the conservatory and then try again, or they may turn to one of the less demanding musical careers which require only a three-year training program.

One such three-year program is offered in the same six conservatories that offer secondary school music majors. This three-year program is a college level one, to follow the four-year secondary program, and leads to a teachers' diploma. It certifies the three-year graduate to teach an instrument and *sol-fa* in the special music preparatory schools and centers for instrumental study mentioned earlier, or to teach music in the General Primary and Secondary Schools. The official title of these institutes housed in the conservatories is "Teacher-Training Colleges for Singing and Music." These recently became affiliates of the Liszt Academy of Music.

Those accepted by the Academy will train to become concert artists, musicologists, conductors, composers, choir directors, and teachers. It is interesting to note that a higher level of musicianship is required of the teacher-training candidates in their entrance examinations than of the artist-training candidates. It is largely from this small group of Academy-trained teachers that the Singing Primary and Secondary Schools are staffed.

The Franz Liszt Academy of Music is a five-year school of university level with departments in Composition, Musicology, Piano, Strings, Woodwinds, Voice, and Pedagogy. The curriculum is designed to cover all the traditional aspects of music as well as to meet the needs of the musician in the modern world. Special emphasis is given, in all depart-ments, to the study of Hungarian music, folk and composed. A violin major in his second year, for example, might have two one-hour lessons a week on violin, one hour of string quartet, four hours of orchestra, one hour of a second string instrument, a half hour of piano, two hours of ear training, two hours of choir, two hours of music theory, and two hours of music history, in addition to the two required hours of social sciences and two of Russian. In other years his schedule would be similar but would include the history of Hungarian music, or Hungarian folk music. If he wished to teach his instrument he would be required, in addition, to take courses in pedagogy and to do practice teaching.

The teacher-training candidate at the Academy has an equally intense training. His program for the third year, for example, includes one hour a week of methods of teaching, two hours of the pedagogy of the Kodály Method (*not* listed this way in Hungary), three of choir conducting, five of teaching practice, a half hour of transposition and score reading, one hour of his instrument, a half hour of voice study, two hours of ear training, two of choir, four of music theory, two of music history, and two of social sciences. In other years he studies, in addition, speech theory, history of instruments, adult education, Hungarian folk music, the aesthetics of music, and Russian (two years).

For his practice teaching he works in a General Primary School during his third Academy year, in a Singing Primary School during his fourth year, and in a secondary school during his fifth year. His practice teach-ing is closely guided by the master teacher with whom he works and by the Academy supervisor of student teachers. He is expected to follow the normal teaching syllabus for his practice classes.

At the end of five satisfactory years the student receives a diploma which accredits him for teaching at any level from the general primary up through the conservatory. His placement depends upon the available openings and his own abilities. He is expected to teach about twenty-four periods a week and to involve himself in any way he can in the musical life of his community, through organizing and conducting a choir or orchestra, for example, or by working with the *Jeunesses Musicales* (an international organization of which Hungary is a member).

Before leaving the field of college education, it is necessary to mention the training of classroom teachers, since these teachers are responsible for music education in the first four grades of most General Primary Schools. The Ministry of Education has been aware for some time of the difficulties involved in upgrading music education with teachers who themselves are inadequately trained in music. It is a difficult task to retrain teachers who have been in the system for many years, but effort is being expended in this direction via in-service meetings and short courses. In the training of new teachers, care is taken to select the more musically able candidates for the early grades, and musical training occupies a large place in the curricula of the three- and four-year teacher-training colleges. *Sol-fa,* the pedagogy of the Method, piano, and music history are given during the three hours a week of compulsory music, in addition to two required hours of choir participation.

There are three four-year colleges located at Pécs, Egér, and Széged, which prepare teachers for the upper grades of the General Primary School. In order to teach grades 5 to 8 the teacher must specialize in two areas chosen from mathematics, history, Hungarian, music, and foreign languages. For the teacher who chooses music and one other subject, music is treated as any major area of study. *Sol-fa* is given for two hours a week throughout the four years, and instrumental study, singing, score reading, and choral work all occupy a prominent place in the curriculum, in addition to the usual pedagogy of courses and required practice teaching.

Naturally, the graduates of these three- and four-year teacher-training institutes do not possess the musical backgrounds of the graduates in teacher-training from the conservatories or from the Liszt Academy. But if their musical training is compared, instead, with that provided by the usual American teacher-training institute, the quality and quantity of such training received by the Hungarian teacher-training candidate are astounding.

The student who has not chosen music as a profession, but who has perhaps gone through the Singing Primary and Secondary Schools, may continue his musical life at the university level through participation in one of the local choirs or orchestras which abound in every Hungarian town. He will probably not take further music courses if he is majoring in an unrelated field, but he may, of course, study an instrument or voice in one of the centers previously mentioned. The universities do not offer music courses, but such offerings are really unnecessary since the universities are located in cities where there are ample opportunities for extracurricular music study and participation, as, for example, at Széged, Debrecen, and Budapest, where conservatories exist.

One of the most interesting aspects of Hungarian music education is the multiplicity of choices the student has at every level. He may enter a Singing Primary or a General Primary School. He may take solfege and music theory in the music preparatory school, beginning at age seven or eight, and begin instrumental lessons at an instrumental study center two years later if he so desires. He may attend a General Secondary School, a General Secondary School with Emphasis in Music, or a secondary school affiliated with a conservatory. He may then apply for admission to the Franz Liszt Academy of Music in Budapest, to one of the three-year conservatory programs, or to a three- or four-year teacher-training college. Choices leading to a good music education are possible at every level. Of course, there are entrance requirements along the way, but for the student who fails to meet the entrance requirement to one type of school, there is always an alternative type which also offers good musical education. This broad-based multifaceted system came into existence as a direct result of Zoltan Kodály's conception of comprehensive music education from infant to adult.

chapter 4

The Curriculum: Nursery School through Grade Eight

The Preschool Child and the First Grade in Hungary

More than 60 percent of all Hungarian children begin school at the age of three in nursery schools or day-care centers. In the cities, where both parents usually work, the percentage of three-year-olds in school is even higher. Day-care centers in Hungary are not simply a parent substitute or baby-sitting service but a form of organized preschool education suited to the ages and needs of the children. For them a highly specific and comprehensive curriculum in music has been devised.[1] In general, the aims of music training at the nursery school level are to increase the child's liking for music, to help him sing in tune, to increase his sense of rhythm and beat, and to begin to develop in him a sense of musical discrimination.

Specifically, the youngest children, the three-year-olds, are taught to sing eighteen to twenty songs and singing games, to chant nursery rhymes, to step and clap the beat to duple-meter songs or rhymes, to use hand drums and other simple rhythm instruments, to feel the beat, to learn to distinguish the sounds of drums, cymbals, and triangle, and to hear and respond to soft and loud in music. They are expected to recognize familiar tunes played on xylophone or recorder.

The four-year-olds add another twenty-five or more songs, singing games, and rhymes to their repertory and learn to clap and walk the beat in $\frac{2}{4}$ and $\frac{4}{4}$, distinguishing between accented and unaccented beats. They are introduced to the concepts of high and low and of fast and slow.

---

[1] *Educational Work in Nursery Schools* (Budapest: Ministry of Education, 1957).

The awareness of high and low pitch in music is made visual with hand movements (simply up and down, not the Curwen signs, which are used later). The steps to singing games are used to give emphasis to their rhythmic quality. Children are expected to recognize a familiar tune simply from hearing its clapped rhythm.

The five-year-olds, who correspond in age to kindergarten children in the U.S.A., add still another thirty or so songs to their singing repertory. They continue to develop the concepts of fast-slow, high-low, and loud-soft. Their familiar songs are repeated in a variety of tempi to which they must respond correctly with their tapping, clapping, or stepping. They are expected to be able to clap the rhythm of a familiar song without singing it simply by inner-hearing, and to echo-clap simple two-bar duple-meter rhythm patterns both in groups and individually. All songs are taught by rote and no accompaniment is used with the singing other than occasional rhythm instruments.

Throughout the three years of nursery school great stress is laid on individual response, both rhythmical and melodical. Individual work is considered necessary to ensure correct singing. At the end of this three-year period the six-year-old in Hungary can usually step the beat and clap the rhythm correctly to any of the songs in his repertory. He can, as a rule, sing most of those songs in tune from memory. He understands the musical concepts of high-low, loud-soft, and fast-slow, and can demonstrate his understanding behaviorally.

It is obvious that the teachers for such schools must have a strong musical background, and they do. No student is accepted into a kindergarten-teaching-training institute who does not exhibit above-average musical ability. In addition, music instruction comprises a major portion of the kindergarten teachers' training. They are given weekly instruction in singing, *sol-fa*, ear training, and an instrument, as well as being required to sing in a choir.

The program described in the preceding pages is for the "General Nursery Schools." There are, in addition, about one hundred special "Music Nursery Schools," generally located near the Singing Primary Schools. These devote more time weekly to music than do the General Nursery Schools, and provide a more intensive program for skill and concept building. All singing is, however, still rote-learned. No attempt is made to push children into music reading at such an early age. The work done in these Music Nursery Schools could best be described as providing a more total musical environment for the children, and, perhaps, touching on musical reading readiness, to the extent of attaching specific hand signs to the notes of the pentaton and using some *sol-fa* syllables in known songs.

The gap between what is taught in the Music Nursery and the General Nursery Schools has narrowed considerably in recent years. According to Katalin Forrai, Director of all preschool music in Hungary, the eventual aim is to have all nursery schools be essentially music nursery schools. Only an insufficient number of trained teachers at present delays the implementation of this goal.

Grade One in Hungary

In the first-grade Singing School class in Hungary the children have music five to six times a week, for a total of 165 lessons during the school year. They learn 80 songs—folk songs, singing games, children's songs. Most of these are taught by rote, but some are taught by hand signs and, toward the end of the year, some are read from staff notation. As in any good music class, attention is given to clear articulation of words, correct posture and breathing, and expressive singing. The concepts taught in the nursery school about fast-slow, loud-soft, and high-low, are reintroduced and reinforced. As in the nursery school the children continue to step the beat and clap the rhythm to many duple-meter songs, both while singing and while practicing "inner-hearing," i.e., thinking the tune, stepping the beat, clapping the rhythm, *without* singing.

Simple one- or two-measure duple-meter ostinati (e.g., | ⊓ | ⟩ or | | ⊓ |) are introduced, to be clapped while singing well-known songs. Easy melodic canons are introduced.

The specific teaching material of the grade is, in rhythm, quarter notes (|), eighth notes in groupings of two and four (⊓ or ⊓⊓), ta — ti ti — ti ti ti ti — quarter rests (⟩ , written as ⦚ in Hungary), half notes (♩) and ta — 1 2 half note rests (2 beats silence), and two-four time ($\frac{2}{4}$) for which only a partial time signature is shown in the children's book, namely, (2).

In melodic learning, first-grade children are taught to identify, sing, write, and read the tones of the pentaton with *sol-fa* syllables and the Curwen hand sings, beginning with *so-mi,* the minor third; then adding *la,* the second or fourth above the two known notes; then *do,* the tonal center; and *re.* Low *la* and low *so* are taught last. As each new note is introduced, all tonal patterns containing this note and the previously-learned ones are shown in three key placements: C, F, and G. Each of these tonal patterns is drawn from known song material and all reading and writing music material is restricted to these three keys in the first grade.

In addition, the repeat sign ‖: :‖ and the fermata ⌒ are taught in first grade. By the end of the year the children are expected to be able to sing eighty songs accurately from memory, to repeat melodic or rhythmic motifs, and to read selected materials with only the notes of the pentaton present. They are also expected to be able to take melodic and rhythmic dictation within the same simple range and with familiar rhythm patterns.

If this sounds like an impossibly ambitious program for a six-year-old, the fact remains that the author has observed it being accomplished, and accomplished well, in the Singing Primary Schools of Hungary. The children participating in it seem happy and under no strain. They show no signs of being pushed beyond their capabilities, of being frustrated or bored by the work expected of them. On the contrary, great enthusiasm is shown for each new skill, each new step along the way.

Grade Two in Hungary

Much time is spent at the beginning of second grade reinforcing the material taught in grade one. The first fifty pages of the music text are a review of the skills and concepts previously taught.

An additional eighty songs are added to the repertory in second grade. One of the essential ingredients of the Kodály Method is a continually growing repertory of song material from which the skill and concept learnings are drawn. It is not uncommon in third grade to return to a song taught in the first, to make conscious a particular new rhythm or tonal pattern. It is this ever-growing core of familiar music that comprises the basic teaching material of the Method.

The songs used in second grade are still specifically Hungarian in character: singing games, nursery songs, and folk songs, with some composed music in simple range and folk style.

From this music, the specific teaching material for the second grade is, in rhythm:

The whole note **o** and the whole note rest ▬ ,

Four-four $\left(\frac{4}{4}\right)$ and three-four $\left(\frac{3}{4}\right)$ meter,

The dotted half note 𝅗𝅥. ,

Syncopation ♪ ♩ ♪,

The eighth rest 𝄾 ,

Dotted rhythm patterns ♪ 𝅗𝅥. and 𝅗𝅥. ♪ .

The syncopated and dotted rhythm patterns abound in Hungarian folk music and so are not difficult for Hungarian children.

The melodic teaching for the grade includes:

1. Use of leger lines,
2. Upper *re* and *mi* (*r'* and *m'*),
3. New scale steps *fa* and *ti*,
4. Introduction to absolute names of the notes (A B C D E F G).

The C, F, and G *do*'s already in the children's reading vocabulary are taught as specific keys and their signatures are introduced when needed —e.g., the B♭ in the key of F becomes necessary only when *fa* is taught. In a pentatonic scale built on F, no key signature is necessary. Similarly, the F♯ in the key of G becomes necessary for the *ti* in that major diatonic scale or in the *la* minor scale beginning on E.

The slur (⌣) is presented, and the concept of legato singing is stressed. Two-, three-, and four-part canons are sung. The creative process is encouraged through both rhythmic and melodic improvisation in question and answer form. Short improvised melodies and rhythms are used as ostinati with familiar songs.

Songs learned by rote in first grade are now sung both in *sol-fa* and with letter names from music. There is also *prima vista* sight-singing of songs in the scales now well known to the children, i.e., in:

	Major	*Minor*
The Pentaton	*d r m s l*	*l‚ d r m s*
The Pentachord	*d r m f s*	*l‚ t‚ d r m*
The Hexachord	*d r m f s l*	*l‚ t‚ d r m f*

Although the children have learned all of the notes of the diatonic major (*d r m f s l t d*) and of the pure minor scale (*l‚ t‚ d r m f s l*), relatively little song material in the second grade is based on these scales.

Children learn to determine the form of simple folk songs in terms of like and different melodic phrases. They also spend a part of each music period improving their skill in music writing, both through melodic dictation and by reconstructing familiar songs from memory.

There is continued emphasis on the musical quality of the singing. Individual voice help is a part of each lesson.

Grade Three in Hungary

In grade three again eighty songs or more are taught. Up to this time the song material has been almost exclusively Hungarian, in keeping with Kodály's often expressed belief that in music, as in speech, the first language should be the mother tongue. However, beginning in third grade some folk songs of other nations are included.

The new teaching material for the grade includes:

Sixteenth notes in groupings of two and four (𝄶 𝄶 𝄶),

Alternating measures of $\frac{2}{4}$ and $\frac{4}{4}$ in the same song,

The new keys of D and B♭ as *do*,

Singing and identification by name of perfect, major, and minor intervals (for example, the child sings *"so-mi*, G-E, minor-third":

Classification by ear and by sight of songs as belonging to major or minor scale types,

Continued practice in reading and writing music, using the learned musical vocabulary in increasingly difficult material.

It may be seen from this that by the end of third grade the Hungarian Singing-School child is, for all practical purposes, musically literate. There is still a vast amount of musical material left to discover, but the basic skills necessary to reading, writing, and singing music have become a part of the child.

Grade Four in Hungary

The expanding song repertory now begins to include more folk material of other countries and cultures, along with good composed music of the best of the Hungarian composers and the songs of Mozart, Haydn, and Cherubini.

New rhythmic material includes:

Triplets (⌐⌐⌐₃ ⌐⌐⌐₃),

Combinations of dotted eighths and sixteenth (𝅘𝅥𝅯. and .𝅘𝅥𝅯),

$\frac{2}{8}, \frac{4}{8}, \frac{3}{8},$ and $\frac{6}{8}$ meters (taught in that order).

It is interesting to note that there is almost no Hungarian folk music in $\frac{6}{8}$ meter and that Hungarian children find this a difficult meter to master. American and Western European folk music, on the other hand, is full of examples of $\frac{6}{8}$.

In melodic learning the new material for grade four is:

E♭ and A♭ *do* with their associated major and minor scales,
Folk song form—children are expected to be able to diagram the form of familiar folk songs.

Some attempt is made to begin *prima-vista* sight-singing using words instead of *sol-fa* syllables. This, of course, presents an added level of difficulty since the child must now grasp the words printed under the staff and the musical notation on the staff simultaneously. Up to this time, either the text has been taught by rote along with the melody, or the song has been read in *sol-fa* first and the words added later. In general, however, syllables are still used extensively for first reading of new material even at the university and music academy level.

Music writing continues in the known keys and scales and, generally, is still taken from known musical material. In addition to the familiar major and minor scales, Dorian, Phrygian, and Mixolydian modes are introduced through folk songs, and the scales associated with these modes are learned:

la (minor or Aeolian),
do (major, or Ionian)
re (Dorian),
mi (Phrygian),
so (Mixolydian).

The modes are not necessarily referred to by their names at this time. They may be simply mentioned as "the scale on *re*," *r m f s l t d' r'* (Dorian).

Grade Five in Hungary

In fifth grade some sixty songs are taught, ranging from Hungarian folk and art songs to the European masters, with great emphasis on canons and polyphonic music. About half of this song material is still taught first by rote. Of the rote material, children later notate ten to fifteen songs in their staff books by ear.

Common time (C) and cut-time (¢) are introduced and compound meter is reinforced. More heterometric songs are taught, i.e., songs with $\frac{2}{4}$ and $\frac{3}{4}$ or other such combinations of meters. The relationship of major and minor scales is investigated through singing and analyzing them. E *do* and A♭ *do* are introduced with their related minors. Inversions of perfect, major, and minor intervals are sung, studied, and written. Music listening is a regular part of the lesson, with emphasis on the works of Hungarian composers.

Grade Six in Hungary

The song material of the sixth grade is widely varied, beginning with ancient Hungarian folk songs and a detailed study of old and new styles in folk music. From this the children move through three centuries of European and English composed music. They begin with the sixteenth-century composers Josquin Des Pres and Orlando de Lassus, singing their works and those of Morley, Telemann, Purcell, Bach, Handel, Mozart, Haydn, and Beethoven. This, clearly, is the level at which the skills gathered in the previous five years are put to work with the best of music literature. Children do not simply listen to, but also sing, the works of the finest of three centuries of music. The music of these great composers is sung and analyzed for form, chord structure, and style. Musical dictation is now expanded to include known motifs by the Baroque and Classical composers. As at every grade level, a musically beautiful rendition of the song material is considered of first importance.

Grades Seven and Eight in Hungary

The Hungarian Singing Primary School is an eight-year school. The work of the last two years is of only academic interest here in the U.S.A., where the elementary is typically a five- or six-year school and where it will rarely be possible to accomplish even the full six-year Hungarian program. However, the expectation of Hungarian children in seventh and eighth grades, briefly, is:

Singing of all major, minor, and modal scales up to six sharps and flats, in *sol-fa* and in absolute note names,

Knowing and singing all inversions of triads in major and minor keys,

Familiarity with the musical forms of song, aria, madrigal, cantata, symphony, and opera,

Study of music of the nineteenth- and twentieth-century composers through singing, listening, analysis, and writing.

Conclusion

The child in Hungary who enters nursery school at three or four years of age and then attends one of the 130 or so Singing Primary Schools for his eight years of elementary education, achieves a level of musical competency rare in the U.S.A., even among trained musicians. His musical skills, while often applied to instrumental study, are not primarily instrumentally oriented, but are broad-based, preparing him for a wide range of musical experiences. His eight years plus of music training have made of him a knowledgeable, musically literate amateur. This was Kodály's aim.

part 2

Kodály for American Schools

chapter 5

Kodály for American Schools:
Grade One

The scope of the eight-year music program in Hungary includes a formidable amount of teaching material when thought of in terms of the typical American school situation of music once or twice a week. However, the sequence of the Kodály Method is a valid one, and it is possible to accomplish much through it in the six years of American elementary school. That the basic skills of music literacy can be taught through the Kodály Method to American children has been demonstrated in a number of schools from New England to California.

It is necessary to mention at the outset that the only way anything sequential can be taught to six-year-olds in a once-a-week lesson is by having the full cooperation of the classroom teacher. She must attend all lessons and follow them with regular practice. There is too great a time gap from one week to the next to expect success from a sequential program with young children on a once-a-week basis. Twice a week makes the continuity of the sequence possible, and twice a week with reinforcement by the classroom teacher is even better.

The implications of this for scheduling are obvious. Two twenty-minute periods with first grade are far more valuable than one forty-minute period. The length of the period is not so important as the frequency. In the first three grades, where the whole foundation of musical knowledge is laid, it is important that the music specialist have at least two lessons a week with each class.

What is a Feasible Program
for Grade One in American Schools?

In the U.S.A. we have no comprehensive preschool training for children. Public nursery schools for three- and four-year-olds are all but unheard of, and many sections of the country do not even have public kindergartens for the five- and six-year-olds. It is obvious, then, that the work of the nursery schools of Hungary must be accomplished in first grade in American schools. This is not as disadvantageous as it seems upon first consideration. The six-year-old is obviously more mature and more ready to learn than the three- or four-year-old, and he learns at a faster rate. It is within the realm of possibility for an American first grade to accomplish what is accomplished in Hungary in the three nursery school years, as well as to acquire some, but not all, of the skill and concept learning of the first grade in Hungary.

What, specifically, can be accomplished with first graders in the framework of the Kodály Method? First, it is necessary to teach the concepts and skills normally covered in the Hungarian Nursery School, i.e., in-tune singing, feeling for beat and accent in duple meter, ability to identify rhythm patterns of familiar songs and to step and clap rhythm and beat, as well as the understanding of the concepts of high-low, loud-soft, and fast-slow. In addition, it is necessary to build a repertory of songs and singing games of small range and easy rhythms from which to draw the later skill-teaching material. Some of these the children may already know when they come to school. Others will have to be taught.

Two familiar nursery rhymes, good for teaching duple meter and later for deriving rhythm pattern and accent, are

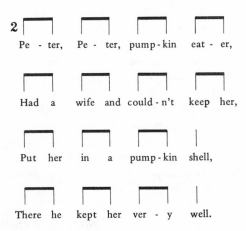

and

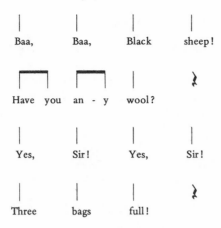

Baa,   Baa,   Black   sheep!

Have   you   an - y   wool?

Yes,   Sir!   Yes,   Sir!

Three   bags   full!

Children may 1) say these in rhythm, 2) step the beat, 3) clap the rhythm (the way the words go), 4) play the rhythm on hand drum or rhythm sticks while stepping the beat, and 5) clap the rhythm while thinking the words but not saying them aloud. These activities, in order of increasing difficulty, aid in the development of a rhythmic sense as well as of inner hearing and concentration.

Concurrently with training in rhythm and beat, attention must be given to in-tune singing. It is essential that there be much individual singing and tone matching in first grade. One simple way to encourage each child to match pitch is to have him sing his name, echoing the teacher on a *so-mi* or *so-mi-la* pattern.

Example:

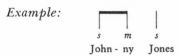

s   m   s
John - ny   Jones

Later the teacher may sing questions to which the child creates an answer:

Teacher:

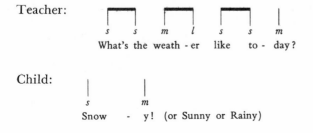

s   s   m   l   s   s   m
What's the weath - er   like   to - day?

Child:

s   m
Snow   -   y!   (or Sunny or Rainy)

The simpler the required response, the more likely the child with pitch problems is to sing it correctly. In working with an individual child with a pitch problem the teacher should ask him to sing softly so that the child can hear the teacher's voice along with his. Often, out-of-tune singers sing so loudly they cannot hear others and so are unaware that they are not in tune. Of course, it goes without saying that never, under any circumstances, should an out-of-tune singer be discouraged from singing. Some children require more time to find their voices than others, but if there is no physiological disability in hearing or speech, any child can be taught to sing correctly in tune. In three prolonged visits to Hungary the author never heard an out-of-tune singer above second grade.

The earliest material used for teaching children to sing accurately and in tune should be authentic children's singing games and folk music of the proper ambit, i.e., within the range of the pentaton centering around F or F♯. F♯ was found to be the usual center tone children chose when singing independently.[1] The half step *fa-mi* will occur in some of the material, since many American children's songs contain a descending line at the end: *s f m r d,* making the song pentachordal, or, *l s f m r d,* making it hexachordal. However, the bulk of the teaching material should omit the half steps *fa* and *ti,* since research has shown that they are difficult for young children to sing in tune.[2]

The songs taught at this point by rote will be used later for making specific tonal and rhythm patterns conscious to the children, so it is important to keep in mind the possible future pedagogical use of the material when choosing it. For example, the three-note song "Bye, Baby Bunting" may be used for several teaching purposes:

Bye,   Bab - y   Bunt - ing,   etc.

The children may use a rocking motion to show the beat. They may sing the rhythm with rhythm duration syllables: ta ti-ti ta ta. They may find the new note *la* in the song. However, at the initial teaching the song should be taught entirely by rote and its words and soft lullaby quality

1 Gladys Moorhead and Donald Pond, *Music of Young Children* (Santa Barbara, Calif.: Pillsbury Foundation for Advanced Music Education, 1941–1951), Vol. I, Chart, p. 15.

2 Marilyn P. Zimmerman, *Musical Characteristics of Children* (Washington, D.C.: Music Educators National Conference, 1971), pp. 8, 23–26.

emphasized. Only later, when it is well known, should it be put to its other pedagogical uses.

The children's growing repertory of songs should be performed in a variety of ways. In order to reinforce the concepts of high and low, the children might stand and stoop for the obvious high and low sequences in songs; for loud-soft they might perform the same song in a range of dynamics from soft to loud, or, in the case of a march, step softly as if the parade were far away, then louder as it approaches, then very loud as it reaches the reviewing stand. The same sort of exercise may be done for fast-slow, having the children become a train starting slowly, then building up speed, and finally slowing down to a stop as they come into the station. Later it is useful to combine concepts. Ask a child to play the drum so that it sounds fast and soft, or the xylophone so that it sounds high and slow.

One half of a school year will in most cases be enough to build a repertory of basic teaching songs, to develop in-tune singing, and to ensure that the children demonstrate understanding of the basic music concepts. When, and only when, these basic skills are behaviorally observable is it time to move into the teaching sequence of the method. It should go without saying that for a child who cannot sing a minor third accurately to call what he *is* singing *so-mi* is patently absurd.

The first rhythmic and melodic patterns made specifically conscious to children are those from their own singing games and songs. As it happens, these are quite closely related in melodic and rhythmic structure to those taught in Hungary and, indeed, to early childhood songs all over the world. Our simplest children's song material is based on the minor third (*so-mi*), often with the addition of an unstressed beat of the fourth above the *mi, la*. One Hungarian children's song, for example, goes:

s	*m*	*s*	*s*	*m*
Zip,	Zup,	Ken -	der	Zup.

This is identical to the American children's song:

s	*m*	*s*	*s*	*m*
Rain,	Rain,	Go	A -	way.

The American children's chant "One, Two, Tie My Shoe," sung by children entirely on *so-mi,* gives repeatedly the rhythm pattern

| | | ⌐ | |
| ta | ta | ti - ti | ta |

like the opening phrase of the Hungarian children's songs

		⌐	
Hint - a	Pa - lin	ta
Re - tes	Ke - re - kes

Two other familiar duple-meter songs of limited range and simple rhythm are "Ring Around the Rosy" and "Lucy Locket, Lost Her Pocket." These songs and others of equal simplicity should be taught early in the year. They are excellent aids to in-tune singing, and once they have been thoroughly learned, they may be used to make conscious the rhythm patterns of | ⌐¬ and ⸰ to the children, as well as the
ta   ti - ti   rest
tonal patterns of *so-mi-la.*

When the children are able to step the beat accurately they may be told that the beat note is called "ta" and looks like this: | | | |
ta ta ta ta

Because they have been clapping the beat and rhythm for some time before this, it is a simple matter for the children to discern where there are two sounds on one beat in a familiar song. It is sometimes useful to have children physically demonstrate the rhythm of the song by having one child group others into the rhythm pattern:

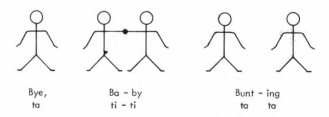

| Bye, | Ba – by | Bunt – ing |
| ta | ti – ti | ta   ta |

Where they see and hear the two sounds on one beat, the sounds are

called "ti-ti" and are written  . The ta's and ti's may then be sung
as an additional verse to familiar duple-meter songs.

Writing or constructing known rhythm patterns should begin as soon
as children are familiar with the symbols | ta and | | ti - ti . Since many
first grade children are not facile with pencil and paper, bundles of
sticks provide a simple and quick means for them to take rhythmic
dictation. Thin dowels may be cut to five-inch lengths and arranged in
bundles of twenty or so per child. They have the advantage of being
more visible at a glance to the teacher than paper and pencil work.
Such rhythm pattern sticks are used in Hungary and are available com-
mercially in the U.S.

One procedure for such rhythm dictation in first grade might be for
the class to 1) sing the song with words, 2) repeat it singing ta's and ti's,
3) construct the pattern they have just sung with the rhythm pattern
sticks:

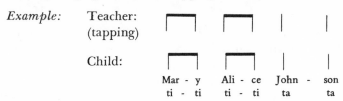

4) sing the song again, this time pointing to the sticks.

An intermediate step which may prove helpful for the child who en-
counters difficulty is to have him tap the song rhythm, moving his hand
across the desk from left to right. This will give him the exact placement for his pattern sticks.

For additional practice in identifying rhythms there are some useful
games. As the teacher has sung children's names when working on in-
tune singing, she may now tap the rhythm of a child's name. He should
answer by singing his name, clapping the rhythm.

Example: Teacher:
(tapping)

Child:

Mar - y	Ali - ce	John -	son
ti - ti	ti - ti	ta	ta

Or the class may identify the child by the name-rhythm and give the response.

The disk game provides practice in differentiating between rhythm and beat:

Children sing and clap the beat of a familiar song.

When the teacher holds up a red disk the children switch to clapping the rhythm.

When she holds up a blue disk, they return to the beat.

The disks should be changed several times during the song. Again, the teacher may simply clap the rhythm of a familiar song and ask the children what it is. When they have become proficient at this, individual children may take the place of the teacher.

After ta and ti-ti, the quarter rest may be introduced either through a familiar song or through a nursery rhyme. "Peas Porridge Hot" is a good one:

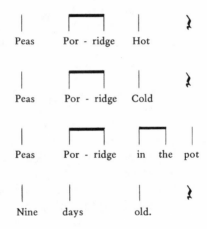

The rest is taught as one beat of silence. When clapping a rhythm pattern, the children should make a forceful but silent motion with the hands for the rest. They may tap their shoulders or simply swing their arms out, but the feeling of a definite beat must be there. In Hungary the rest is drawn simply as a ∠. The usual manuscript rest sign ⅃ is no more difficult for children, and may be constructed with sticks or drawn with little difficulty.

Once the quarter note, eighth note, and rest symbols have been thoroughly learned, the repeat may be introduced. Children will readily grasp the idea that by placing a sign after a measure or a phrase they can avoid writing or constructing it twice. They may use the sign even when responding orally by saying │ │ ┌─┐ │ and then making
              ta   ta ti - ti   ta
the repeat sign :‖ in the air with two fingers.

The concept of measure takes a little longer, but it should be included in first grade. When it is observable that the children understand beat to be the steady underlying pulse of songs and rhythm to be the group-ings of longer and shorter sounds and silences over the beat, the concept that music has accented and unaccented beats may be introduced. This may be done by the teacher singing a duple-meter song, stressing the accented beats. Children should be asked whether all the beats sound the same. They will hear that some beats are louder than others. They can feel the accented beats by marching, stepping heavily on the louder beats. One child might go to the board and draw the beats as the teacher sings. He should be instructed to show that some beats are louder than others. The pattern he will probably draw is the following one, or some variation thereof:

The teacher can then explain that it is not possible to have some ta's large and some small; that in music there are accent marks to show where the loud ta's are,

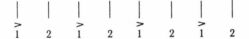

and that in counting beats the accented beat is always "1."

There should be some practice with this before proceeding to bar lines and measures, but once the concept of regular accented and unac-cented beats is understood, it is a short step to the function of the bar line. It may be explained to children that to make music easier to read, musicians draw lines before each accented beat. The space between these lines is known as a "measure," and the number of beats in a measure is always shown at the beginning of a song:

This should be done only with the most common meter of children's songs—the duple meter—in first grade. That is not to say that only duple-meter songs should be taught in first grade. On the contrary, it is essen-tial to teach some songs in $\frac{3}{4}$, $\frac{4}{4}$, and $\frac{6}{8}$, since so much of American musical heritage lies in these meters. These rhythmically more complicated songs, if taught by rote in first grade, may be used in later grades for skill teaching. However, the skill teaching material of first grade should be restricted to $\frac{2}{4}$. That duple meter is the basic meter of early childhood has been demonstrated in numerous experimental studies of which The Pillsbury Report was one of the earliest.[3] Only by obtaining a firm foundation in duple meter will the child later be able to comprehend more complicated metric patterns.

When the children are able to sing their simplest songs in tune, and have learned the rhythm syllables for quarter-note and eighth-note rhythms, they are ready to begin melodic interval learning. The first interval, the minor third *so-mi,* should be introduced through a familiar song. The interval must be taught by its sound or tune, identified with the syllables, *so-mi,* practiced with hand signs, and shown in position on the staff. For example: for

the children sing, first: One, two, tie my shoe

then: *s   m   s*   s   m

then show with hands while singing:

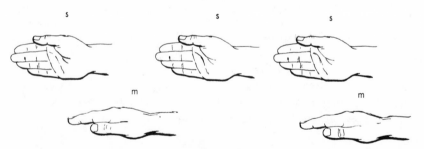

Before the position of *so-mi* on the staff can be taught, it is necessary to spend one or two lessons helping the children become familiar with the musical staff and the terminology associated with it. For this, felt staves of a size to fit comfortably on each child's desk are invaluable. Both felt staves and magnetic staff boards are common in Hungarian schools. Here felt staves may be made easily and inexpensively out of cut

[3] Moorhead and Pond, Volume I, Chart, p. 12.

felt and staff-lined with magic marker or stitching. Each staff should have an envelope of stemless notes attached. There are commercial magnetic music staff boards available here, but to date all are too complicated, with stemmed notes, G-clefs, sharps, flats, etc. They could be useful in fourth grade, but not in first.

The first fact that children should be led to discover is that the staff has five lines. They must be told that the lines of a staff are counted from the bottom up, like climbing a ladder; the child's natural tendency is to count from the top down, as he would number a spelling paper.

The next step is to define what is meant by "on a line" when referring to the staff. In writing their names, children write the letters sitting on top of the line, but a note "on the line" must have the line running directly through it. This must be learned and practiced with felt staves or individual magnetic staff boards. A game can be made of it, combining the idea of "on a line" with the idea of counting staff lines from bottom to top. The children take one note from their envelopes and as the teacher calls "fourth line, first line, third line," each child places his note on the staff.

After the children have become facile in placing notes correctly on lines, they may be asked if they see any other places on the staff where there is room for notes. Usually they see the "places between the lines." These are introduced as spaces, and the same game procedure is followed as for lines.

All of this simply enables children to move notes correctly and with facility on the lines and spaces of the staff. It is a necessary step in the development of a musical vocabulary, but there is no real musical learning involved, since at no time in this process is pitch associated with the placement of the note.

After the children are thoroughly familiar with the staff, the association of pitch with specific placement on the staff begins with writing or with constructing on felt staves the pattern *so-mi*, which is known through the song material. This pattern should be drawn from a familiar song, the specific *s-m* pattern isolated, and its position on the staff shown on the chalkboard and constructed on individual staves by the children. The teacher may find that children perceive the space-to-space *so-mi* pattern more easily than the line-to-line one in placing the notes on the staff.

Once introduced, the interval must be reinforced through additional songs. New song material may be read by the children from the board or from teacher-made charts, or may be taught by rote and the rhythmic and melodic notation derived by the class. With teacher guidance the derived notation may be constructed on felt staves or written on the chalkboard.

One order for deriving such a melodic and rhythmic notation might be as follows:

The children

1. Sing the song with words, clapping the rhythm:

2. Sing the song again, this time with rhythm duration syllables:

3. Derive the rhythm at desks with sticks.
4. Place rhythm on blackboard in stick notation:

5. Sing the song again, this time with *so-mi* and hand signs.

The teacher must then place a staff on the blackboard and give the position of *so:*

After this has been done the melody may easily be derived in staff notation on the board and on the individual felt staves.

At some time during the early lessons on the *so-mi* pattern it is helpful for the children to verbalize the rule that:

1. When *so* lives in a space, *mi* lives in the space below;
2. When *so* lives on a line, *mi* lives on the line below.

It must be kept in mind that the interval *s-m* is actually two patterns, one descending, *s-m,* and one ascending, *m-s.* The ascending one is more difficult for children. Care must be taken to provide practice in both patterns through song material selection.

Only when the children are secure in their aural recognition, writing, and singing of the *so-mi* interval should the next new note *la* and its associated patterns be identified for them. The children, of course, will have been singing many songs including the note *la*. From these, one containing only *so, mi,* and *la* should be chosen for deriving the *la*. Ideally, the new pattern should be contained in the first phrase of the basic teaching song.

The intervals to be taught are: *so-la, la-so, mi-la,* and *la-mi.* Each must be taught through known song material and reinforced with new song material. A good introductory song for the *so-la* interval is the children's game "Lucy Locket:"

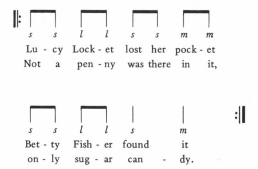

One useful for the *mi-la* interval is

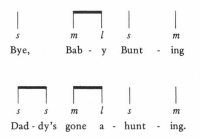

The same procedure should be followed as for teaching the *so-mi* interval. Nothing is intellectualized until it is first known by ear. The process is always 1) auditory to 2) writing or constructing to 3) reading.

This, generally, is as much new material as can be taught successfully to first-grade classes in American schools with music twice a week. The importance of knowing these tonal and rhythm patterns well cannot be too greatly emphasized.

By the end of first grade children should be able to sing familiar two- and three-note songs in tune correctly with words, rhythm duration syllables, *sol-fa* syllables, and hand signs. They should be able to follow the teacher's hand signs, hearing mentally the tune she is making. They should be able to do simple two-hand singing—i.e., when the teacher shows *mi* with one hand and *so-la-so* with the other, the class, divided into two groups, should follow—one group singing the *mi* while the other sings *so-la-so*. It is important that they hear intervals in this fashion —one note with the other. The children should be able to write or construct with felt staves and sticks any of the songs within their three-note reading repertory.

With all, they must never be given the feeling that music is mechanical. Each lesson must be a musical experience. To this end, dynamics and phrasing must be considered in all singing, and attention must be given to singing in a variety of tempi. Games which accompany the songs should be played frequently. To the children, they are the reason for the songs. There is little point in giving children the skills with which to understand music if at the same time they are not given the opportunity to enjoy making music.

chapter 6

Kódaly for American Schools:
Grade Two

In his original conception of the method, Kodály considered that one of the strengths of the movable-*do* as a tool was that it did not restrict vocal sight-singing to key. The minor third, *so-mi,* is identified by its intervallic relationship, its sound, its function in the scale of the song in question, and its placement on the staff: space-space or line-line in *any* key. This was a simple enough concept, he thought, for children to grasp. He considered it unnecessary and undesirable in an approach aimed at vocal musical literacy to restrict young children to specific keys. A child knowing only the five tones of the pentaton, *do, re, mi, so, la,* could read them in any placement on the staff and in any clef, once told where *do* was. His idea was to reduce the complex musical page to the simplest musical elements, while still enabling children to read patterns encompassing the entire staff.

In recent years, however, a change has taken place in the official curriculum as practiced by teachers throughout Hungary. Today children in grades one and two are restricted to the keys of C, F, and G. All their reading and writing exercises are in these three keys. One rationale given for this change in procedure is that students need a firm key-centered foundation as preparation for instrumental music reading. Since the Kodály Method was never intended to be one primarily of preparation for instrumental study but, rather, a vocal method aimed at universal music literacy, this insistence on key-centeredness seems out of character. It is doubtful that the advantage of easier instrumental reading at third or fourth grade is worth the inhibition of a wider range of vocal reading in the lower grades.

There may be, however, a more valid reason for restricting early instruction to the keys of C, F, and G. In these keys no key signature is required for pentatonic songs. The B♭ in the key of F is unnecessary since there is no *fa* in the pentaton; the F♯ in the key of G is unnecessary since there is no *ti*. Therefore, in looking at a musical page the child does not see anything incorrect (such as the absence of a key signature in the key of D where the *mi* would call for a sharp) or see on the page anything he does not understand, as he would if a key signature were to be written but not explained. Key signatures can be taught meaningfully only as the scale half-steps *fa* and *ti* are introduced.

In view of this, perhaps it is best to restrict children's early reading and writing exercises to C, F, and G. Then, when the syllable *fa* is taught in the key of F or the syllable *ti* in the key of G, the one flat or one sharp in the key signature may be introduced in such a way that it has a very real and specific meaning, and is not simply a memorized gimmick, as it so often becomes for beginning music students. In any case, American teachers must decide whether they wish to limit early reading and writing to the keys of C, F, and G or whether they prefer to use the entire staff, simply leaving key signature unexplained until later. In the following chapters it will be assumed that key signature is not introduced until the syllables *fa* and *ti* are taught.

What is a Feasible Program for Grade Two in American Schools?

If the first grade has successfully completed the work outlined, in the second grade the children should be ready to learn the remaining notes of the basic pentaton, *do* and *re,* and to add to their working vocabulary in rhythm, ties, the fermata ⌒ , half notes ♩ , whole notes ta-a-a-a , half and whole note rests ▬▬▬ , and an understanding of $\frac{4}{4}$ meter.

While this seems a small amount of new material, remember that with each new note introduced there is an increasing number of intervals to be taught from the song material. To be correctly taught, each interval must be found in a prominent place in several familiar song examples and then reinforced with new song material. The actual number of intervallic patterns a child must learn for the basic pentaton is twenty:

Tonal Patterns of the Basic Pentaton

New note

s-m	*s-m, m-s*
l	*l-s, s-l, l-m, m-l*
d	*d-s, s-d, d-m, m-d, d-l, l-d*
r	*r-s, s-r, r-m, m-r, r-l, l-r, r-d, d-r*

Each of these intervals must be practiced many times, in the context of song material, and isolated and practiced with hand signs. One tone may be sustained by a part of the class while the others sing the second tone. Only by hearing the two tones together can children develop intervallic hearing. Hand signs should be used by the teacher and by the children in this interval work. Visualization in space is an important aid to correct hearing and singing. The Kodály book "Let Us Sing Correctly" gives many good musical examples of exercises for intervallic training. These may be used by the teacher for reinforcement, but the basic teaching material should be songs.

The first new tone to be taught in second grade is *do,* the tonal center of most folk music of the Western world. A possible preparation song for making *do* conscious to children is "Ring Around the Rosy." It contains only the three notes the children already know, except for the last note of the song: *do.* The actions for the singing game have the children "all fall down" on the final note, physically representing the lower position of the *do* to the *so, la* and *mi* in the song:

To have the children derive the position of *do,* the following singing game is useful since it contains the *do* many times in a strong position:

One Procedure for Introducing do

Both the above-mentioned songs, and many others containing the *do,* should be sung and their games, if any, played. Then the song selected for actually teaching *do* to the class may be:

1. Sung with words.

2. Hummed, with hands indicating relative pitch. The teacher may give the *do* hand sign, but not yet the name or the staff position.

3. Sung in *sol-fa* with hand signs, using *hum* for the unknown note:

4. Placed on the chalkboard in staff notation as follows:

5. Sung, following the staff notation, using hand signs and humming the unknown note.

At this point the teacher may sing the song using the name of the new note, *do*. The children are now ready to sing the entire song from the staff notation on the board. This should be followed by having the children construct the *so-mi-do* pattern on felt staves or on large-lined staff paper.

After the children seem very secure in the sound and position of *do* the teacher should change *so* to the fourth line of the staff and have the class make the necessary changes in *mi* and *do*. It is important to change the singing pitch when changing key this way. Even at a subconscious level children should be helped to associate a note with its actual pitch. If a child is looking at a note in the first space of the treble clef, he should hear that note as F whether its movable *sol-fa* designation is *do, mi, so,* or any other.

After *do* has been presented in a space (key of F) and on a line (key of G) the children should be led to verbalize a rule about the placement of *do*:

1. When *so* and *mi* are in spaces, *do* is in the space below *mi*.
2. When *so* and *mi* are on lines, *do* is on the line below *mi*.

Once this rule is understood, the concept of leger lines may be introduced. When constructing the *so-mi-do* pattern in the key of C, the child can readily see that there is no line for *do*:

However, the rule says *do* must be on a line. The construction of a short line under the staff just for the *do* makes sense to children:

In the lessons that follow there should be much practice identifying *do* in familiar songs. The teacher might sing a song on a neutral syllable, being careful to choose those songs within the cognitive vocabulary of the children, i.e., those containing the notes *do, mi, so,* and *la.* The children, individually and in groups, sing the songs back a phrase at a time, using hand signs and finding *do,* the new note, in each song. The phrase or phrases containing *do* are then constructed on staves. After this, the children should see the song in print in one of their school music books, wherever possible, and should sing from the book using both words and *sol-fa* syllables.

The last step in the procedure is actual music reading. For this the material must be chosen very carefully. It must contain no rhythmic difficulties and no tonal patterns other than those already familiar through known songs, since it is to be a total reading experience in which both rhythm and melody are to be read. If this kind of reading material is not available in the grade singing books the teacher may have to duplicate a song for her class. This is necessary only at the early stages. Once children have all the notes of the extended pentaton, there is some suitable material available in most school song series.

The New Note re

Children may actually derive the position of *re* on the staff. Two good songs for teaching *re* are "Sleep, Baby, Sleep" and "Hot Cross Buns":

a)

b)

Hot Cross Buns! Hot Cross Buns! etc.

One procedure for guiding children to derive *re* is to have them sing a song with rhythm duration syllables and place the rhythm notation on the board with the known *sol-fa* syllables:

After this the class may sing the song, hum the unknown notes, and, following the teacher's example, use the new hand sign for the unknown note:

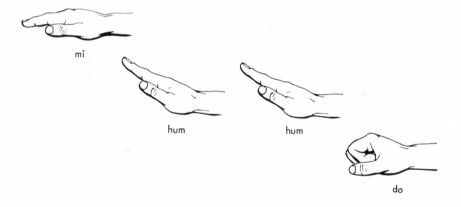

If the teacher then places the known parts of the song on the chalkboard in staff notation, the children, having felt the position of *re* with hand signs, can easily derive its position on the staff.

Once they have discovered the note's place, they may be given its name, *re,* and led to state the rule:

1. If *mi* and *do* are on spaces, *re* is on the line between.
2. If *mi* and *do* are on lines, *re* is on the space between.

It is important that musical examples be used for all the basic pentatonic intervals. Many of these intervals may be found in children's songs and folk songs. However, for some of the less common ones—the fourth from *re* to *so,* or *mi* to *la,* for example—the Kodály Choral Method book "Fifty Nursery Songs" offers some delightful songs for children, specifically composed by Kodály to reinforce the learning of the less common intervals. These small books, intended for use by nursery school teachers in Hungary, could in America provide supplementary music reading material in the pentaton. It is regrettable that the title "Nursery Songs" makes it an impractical volume to hand out to second-grade American children who consider themselves far above the nursery stage. The songs contained in the book are not at all nursery-like in character. For example, the following is an excellent beginning reading song:

(p. 42),

or this one, with its stressed *mi-la* interval:

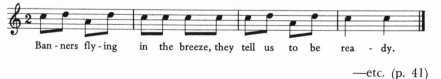

—etc. (p. 41)

In addition to the work on specific intervals, children's inner hearing of melodic line and phrase must be cultivated. This may be aided through various games and exercises. The class could sing a well-known song first with words and then with *sol-fa* syllables and hand signs. At a signal from the teacher the children stop singing but continue thinking the melody and using hand signs. At a second signal from the teacher the class resumes singing aloud. Flash cards may be made of song phrases, from which children can sing the phrase in *sol-fa* and identify the song.

Melodic dictation at this stage should be primarily oral. That is, the teacher sings a melodic phrase on a neutral syllable and the child sings it back in *sol-fa* and with hand signs. There should be much individual work of this kind in second grade. Music writing should be restricted to phrases of well-known songs. If the rhythm and *sol-fa* notation is derived on the chalkboard by teacher and class together, the children should then be able individually to place the notation correctly on the staff. For example:

The teacher might have the children sing "The Closet Key" song first in rhythm duration syllables and then in *sol-fa* and place what they sing on the board:

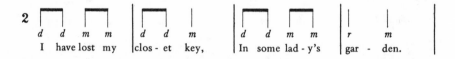

The children should then be able to transfer this notation to staff notation in C, F, or G. In dictation it is important always to use a motif or phrase, never just a measure. Teacher and children must not lose sight of the musical nature of the experience.

Rhythmic Learning

In the rhythm learning material for the grade, $\frac{4}{4}$ meter presents little difficulty. The children have marched, stepped, clapped, and tapped the beat of $\frac{2}{4}$ meter throughout first grade, indicating accented and unaccented beats with their motions. They have demonstrated, without verbalizing, the function of the bar line, i.e., how to define where the stressed beat or accent falls in music. It is important now that they put this understanding into words, so that they may apply it to the new situation—the $\frac{4}{4}$ meter. They may come up with such statements as: *

* The following are actual statements made by second-grade children.

The loud beat is always called "one."

The loud beat always comes right after the bar line.

To count beats in a measure you go from one loud beat until you come to the next loud beat.

When children have shown this level of understanding, the teacher may sing a known $\frac{4}{4}$ song, emphasizing the accented beats slightly more than she would normally.

Example:

Let's   dance the ca - pu - ci - na,   We   have no bread to   eat.   etc.

The children should then sing the song and step the beat, clapping the accented beat, or simply clap the beat as they sing, making the accented beat louder. From this they will be able to derive that there are four beats in a measure. The teacher can show the example on the board, using ta's as beats:

and pointing to them as the children sing the song.

The time signature should be shown on the children's music at this level simply as the number of beats in a measure: two for $\frac{2}{4}$ and four for $\frac{4}{4}$. The bottom number has no meaning for them since the quarter note is the only beat note they know and to them it is "ta." Its mathematical value is not yet relevant to them. One other possible way to write the meter sign so that it will not confuse children is ♩² or ♩⁴ . This can be understood by children as two or four beats in a measure, "ta" being equal to one beat.

Ties and half notes may be introduced through any song with a two-beat note at the end of a phrase, such as "Three Blind Mice." Ask the children to listen and to repeat the rhythm. In most instances the children will at first repeat the rhythm as:

They should be told to listen again to determine whether the teacher's voice really rested on the fourth beat. When they have realized that the tone continues through the fourth beat, the rhythm may be placed on the board with tied quarter notes, so that children may see that there are actually two notes fastened together to make one two-beat sound.

Example:

Later they may be introduced to the half note 𝅗𝅥 as another way of showing two beats of sustained tone:

The song rhythm should again be shown, this time with the half note replacing the tied quarters:

Three blind mice

The rhythm-duration syllable "ta" is extended to two beats for half notes and to four beats for whole notes. There should be no emphasis in the singing on the separate beats of a two- or four-beat ta; the syllable should simply be sung smoothly as the child taps his hand lightly on his desk to maintain the beat.

Example:

Half and whole notes may then be found in familiar songs simply by beat-tapping and determining how many beats a note is sustained. The half and whole rests may be derived in the same manner and their symbols taught.

Whole notes are rare in children's music, and whole rests even rarer.

One possible way to teach the duration of the whole note is through two-hand singing. Following the teacher's hand signs one group might sustain a note for four beats while the second group moves on each quarter note beat:

Many exercises of this sort may be found in the Kodály volume "Let Us Sing Correctly." However, if teaching time is short, since the whole note and the whole rest occur so rarely in children's song material, they can be omitted from the teaching plan until a later grade with little effect on reading ability.

The fermata ⌒ also should be taught in second grade. It may be taught through any song in which the hold is artistically effective. The refrain of "Old Blue" is particularly good for this:

Since the rhythms of this line of this song are not in the cognitive vocabulary of the children, only the "Here, Blue" part should be shown on the board and written by the children:

Much work must be done in this grade to encourage the ability to think, sing, write, and read rhythms correctly. The sticks used in first grade for constructing rhythm patterns may still be used, but the children also should begin to take rhythm dictation with pencil and paper. One procedure for beginning this might be:

1. The teacher sings a familiar song with words in a highly rhythmic fashion while the children listen and think ta's and ti's.

2. The children clap the rhythm and sing the song with ta's and ti's instead of words.

3. The teacher places the complete rhythm notation on the board *as* the children are singing it (for example, "The Closet Key"),

and asks: "How can we change this?"

4. Children will see that a repeat may be used after the fourth bar:

5. The children then read the rhythm from the board in speaking rather than singing voices. (This is always an added problem because children find it difficult to dissociate the rhythm from the known melody. However, this is a necessary step if they are to be able to apply known rhythms to new song material.)

6. The children close their eyes and the teacher erases one measure. The children open their eyes and say the exercise, including the missing measure.

7. The above procedure is repeated until nothing is left on the board and the children are chanting the entire exercise by memory.

8. The children reconstruct the memorized pattern on paper.

Later, when the children have become proficient at this sort of writing exercise, the song rhythm placed on the board may be altered at steps 6 and 7 before being erased. This means that the children would actually be memorizing and writing previously unknown rhythm patterns rather than those drawn from familiar songs.

There should also be frequent aural rhythm dictation in which the teacher claps or taps a pattern of two to four measures in length and the class or an individual child repeats the pattern, clapping and chanting ta's and ti's.

Rhythm flash cards of four beats duration, as used in Hungary, can aid in the development of ability to see rhythm patterns as units rather than in terms of their specific elements. When using flash cards the teacher should show the card only very briefly, then call on individual children to repeat the pattern. This helps in training for musical memory.

As in first grade much attention should be devoted to individual response both in singing and in rhythm work. Each child needs the opportunity to hear himself occasionally without thirty other voices. It helps him to become more aware of his singing voice when he sings alone and when he listens to others sing alone. There should be very few out-of-tune singers left by the end of second grade if the teacher has spent enough time working individually with the children.

Musical form also should be introduced in second grade, to the extent that children should be able to distinguish like and unlike phrases in familiar songs and to diagram these phrases with crayons, as, for example, for an AABA song:

———blue———
———blue———
——— red ———
———blue———

This kind of diagramming may be done for rhythm exercises tapped by the teacher as well as for songs.

Last, but perhaps most important, all song material sung during the year must be performed with attention to the artistry and beauty of the material. It is necessary to take music apart to find where the bar lines go or where the *so-mi* interval occurs, but it is essential to put it back together and to make music of it again in each lesson. A beautiful singing tone, with attention to phrasing and dynamics, must be continually stressed if the music lesson is to be truly musical.

chapter 7

Kodály for American Schools: Grade Three

In third grade the rhythmic learning should include triple meter $\frac{3}{4}$, the dotted half note 𝅗𝅥. , the anacrusis or upbeat, syncopation ♪ ♩ ♪, and the sixteenth-note patterns ♬♬ , ♪♬ , and ♬♪ . In addition, the meaning of the lower numbers in meter signatures should be taught.

In melodic learning the children should be given the remaining notes of the extended pentaton—low *so,* low *la,* high *do.* This will expand the intervallic vocabulary to a possible fifty-six combinations:

Tonal Patterns of the Extended Pentaton

New note

s-m	*s-m, m-s*
l	*l-s, s-l, l-m, m-l*
d	*d-s, s-d, d-m, m-d, d-l, l-d*
r	*r-s, s-r, r-m, m-r, r-l, l-r, r-d, d-r*
l,	*l,-s, s-l,, l,-m, m-l,, l,-l, l-l,, l,-d, d-l,, l,-r, r-l,*
s,	*s,-s, s-s,, s,-m, m-s,, s,-l, l-s,, s,-d, d-s,, s,-r, r-s,, s,-l,, l,-s,*
d'	*d'-s, s-d', d'-m, m-d', d'-l, l-d', d'-d, d-d', d'-r, r-d', d'-l,, l,-d',*
	d'-s,, s,-d'

While some of these intervals are uncommon and unsingable for children, the great majority may be found in folk or composed song material, and must be practiced both through songs and in isolation as intervals.

If absolute note names are to be taught, this is the level at which to begin. The determining factor as to whether or not to teach absolute note names must certainly be teaching time. If there is sufficient teaching time, surely it is good that the children be aware of absolute note names and be able to work with them as they do with *sol-fa*. However, in the teaching situation where there is never enough time to cover the basic grade material, they should be omitted. Absolute note names are unnecessary to vocal sight reading. Given *do,* a singer with a firm *sol-fa* background can read anything placed before him. The purpose of knowing the absolute note names is primarily to prepare for instrumental lessons which commonly begin in the fourth grade. If note names are not taught by the vocal music teacher in third grade, those children who study instruments will learn them later. There is, of course, the advantage of better and more complete musicianship when children know both *sol-fa* syllables and absolute note names. In Hungary the distinction between *sol-fa* syllables and absolute note names in writing is made by using only lower-case letters for the syllables and upper-case ones for the names.

How to Teach Absolute Note Names

If absolute note names are to be taught, they should be introduced early in grade three, much in the same manner as *sol-fa* was introduced in first grade—through well-known songs of very limited range. The first song should be a three-note one on *do-re-mi* in the key of F, one that the children can already read fluently in *sol-fa,* such as "Hot Cross Buns" or "The Closet Key." In these there is a clear stepwise descending *m-r-d* passage.

The teacher may explain to the class that the lines and spaces of the staff have absolute alphabet names as well as the *sol-fa* note names, and that the G-clef always seen in their song books shows which line holds G by curling around the G-line:

Knowing G, the children can discover the note below G as F. They will have to be told that the musical alphabet goes only as high as G and then starts over again. The entire familiar song used to teach A-G-F should then be placed on the chalkboard and sung with words, with *sol-fa,* and with absolute names.

Example:

The singing is an essential step. It is imperative that at this early stage specific pitch be associated with the absolute names. It is a simple matter for a child to memorize F-A-C-E for the spaces and E-G-B-D-F for the lines of the staff, but he should not be allowed to do this. The intellectual knowledge of note names means nothing if it is not accompanied by sure knowledge of relative sounds.

After the children have become proficient at singing their *m-r-d* songs in F with absolute names, the teacher may move on to the key of G, still using only *m-r-d* three-note songs. Only one new note, B, will be needed. Later the procedure should be repeated for the key of C. At this point children will know by both sight and sound the notes from middle C to B. Others may be added as the children seem ready for them.

New Rhythm Learning

Syncopation may be introduced early in grade three through familiar songs. "Sometimes I Feel Like a Mournin' Dove" is excellent for this purpose since the syncopation pattern occurs four times, once at the beginning of each phrase:

The melody and words may be taught by rote. When the children know the song well, the teacher may have them clap the rhythm they are singing. They will hear the pattern but not know its name or rhythm notation. The teacher can then place the rhythm on the chalkboard and give the duration syllables:

sy-co - pa

The syncopated pattern should be taught as a unit of sound so that it will always be recognized and sung as such. Children can easily read the pattern as ti-ta-ti, and read it correctly, but the word "syn-co-pa" presents the pattern as the musical unit it is. The entire song should then be sung by ear with rhythm duration syllables, the children finding where the "syncopa" occurs. Other songs with syncopation should be used in the same way, deriving the new rhythm pattern, clapping it, singing it with duration syllables, and writing it.

Sixteenth notes in groups of four ♫♫ and in combination with eighth notes ♪♫ and ♫♪ may also be introduced early in third grade. A simple but effective folk song for teaching the four sixteenth-note group is "Love Somebody" (the last phrase):

Love   some - bod - y   but   I   won't   say   who!

By tapping the beat while singing, the children can hear that they are singing four sounds on one beat. The pattern can then be placed on the chalk board and the duration syllables given:

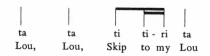

ti - ri - ti - ri

Children should practice singing the song with duration syllables and find similar patterns in other familiar songs. When the children know ti-ti and tiri-tiri, ⌐‾⌐ and ⌐‾‾‾⌐ , well, they can easily derive the patterns ⌐‾‾⌐ and ⌐‾‾⌐ as they find them in songs.

ti   ti- ri   ti- ri   ti

Example: "Skip to My Lou"

ta   ta   ti   ti - ri   ta
Lou,   Lou,   Skip to my   Lou

or

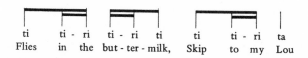

ti   ti - ri   ti - ri   ti   ti   ti - ri   ta
Flies   in   the but - ter - milk,   Skip to   my   Lou

The two most important rhythm learnings for the grade, triple meter and the anacrusis, go hand in hand. Most folk music in $\frac{3}{4}$ begins with an upbeat. However, the initial teaching song for $\frac{3}{4}$ should not contain the upbeat since it adds complications.

One possible beginning triple-meter song without upbeat is the Texan folk song "Billy Barlow":

Let's   go   hunt - ing   says   Risk - y   Rob.

Other possibilities are "Lavender's Blue" and "Oh, How Lovely Is the Evening."

Once they know the song well, children can be led to derive the meter by:

1.   Clapping accented beats louder,
2.   Calling the accented beats "one" and counting the beats between the accented beats.

The rhythm and beats may then be placed on the chalkboard as they are clapped and sung:

One child should place the accent marks under the stressed beats and a second child could draw the bar lines where they belong before the stressed beats. When this much is done, the class can hear and see how many beats there are in a measure, and the number "3" should be placed at the left in the time-signature position.

The completed exercise:

Rhythm:
Beat:

At this point the dotted half note may be introduced, using the same song. Children will feel the three beats of the final note of the song 𝅗𝅥. This can be derived through tied notes:

It is possible that third grade children will have enough comprehension of fractional parts to understand that ♩ is one-half of ♩ and that a dot in music adds one-half the value of the note it follows. However, if this understanding does not come at this time, it is enough that children realize the dotted half, said "ta-a-a," is equal to a two-beat ta tied to a one-beat ta.

While there is American folk music in triple meter, there is less of it than in duple meter or even in $\frac{6}{8}$. The largest number of our triple-meter folk songs seem to be cowboy songs. Most of these start with the anacrusis. As with any musical skill, the anacrusis is best taught aurally. It is more important that the ear hear it as an unstressed beat at the beginning of a song than that the eye simply recognize an incomplete measure.

In this instance the teacher could sing a well-known song two ways—once, correctly stressing the beat after the upbeat, and a second time, incorrectly stressing the first beat of the song. The rhythm notation for the song should be on the chalkboard without bar lines:

The children can decide which version sounds more natural, and, singing the more natural-sounding version, can place accents and bar lines:

They will see that there is only part of a measure at the beginning of the song. They may then be asked to find the rest of the measure. For this they must have the complete song in front of them. Most song series include "Goodbye, Old Paint."

The "4" in $\frac{2}{4}$, $\frac{3}{4}$ and $\frac{4}{4}$ should now be shown on staff notation. The bottom number may be explained as "equal to ta." The children can count and see that $\frac{2}{4}$ means the equivalent of two ta's in a measure, $\frac{3}{4}$, three, and $\frac{4}{4}$, four. The top number means "how many," the bottom number, "what kind." The names "quarter note," "eighth note," "half note," and "whole note" may also be given, although the rhythm duration syllables would still be used in deriving rhythms, since the former are simply names and not durations.

Rhythm dictation exercises now become somewhat longer and more involved. Starting with simple four-beat exercises, the children will gradually develop to the point where by the end of third grade they should be able to retain and repeat accurately exercises of sixteen beats.

An early example of a rhythm tapped by the teacher, to be clapped and chanted back by one child, is:

Later, two well-known rhythm patterns are connected and the child is asked to repeat the eight-beat exercise after the teacher taps it:

The first few times a sixteen-beat exercise is attempted, the last eight beats should be a simple repeat of the first eight:

Only when the children are doing this well should an alteration be made, and then, only one:

↑
alteration

In this way children can be trained to hear and categorize rhythm patterns of considerable length. It is not necessary that such exercises be written by the children. Oral recitation of them and final placement on the chalkboard for the entire class to see and perform are sufficient.

New Tonal Learnings

Low *la* (*l,*) should be the first note of the extended pentaton taught. It should be introduced through a song in which it is the only note unfamiliar to the children—for example, in the last phrase of the four-note children's song "Mister Rabbit":

m   m   d   l,   l,   d
eat-ing all my cab - bage

Since this song contains only *do, re, mi,* and low *la,* it is easy for children to isolate the unknown note and to discover that when *do* is in a space, low *la* is in the space below.

The children may sing the song with words, then with *sol-fa* syllables and hand signs. The sign for low *la* is exactly as for *la* except that the hand is positioned below the *do:*

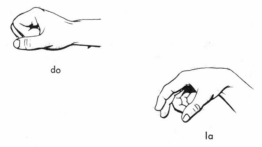

do

la

After singing the song with hand signs the class may derive the rhythm and the *sol-fa* notation on the chalkboard with the help of the teacher:

| ⊓ | ⊓

d d d m m m etc.

From this rhythm and *sol-fa* notation it should be possible for the children to notate the complete song on staff paper in F-, G-, or C-*do*.

It would be well in the follow-up song material to include some minor mode songs. The Southern folk song "I Got a Letter" and "The Indian Canoe Song" are two possibilities. Both have *la,* as the tonal center rather than *do*. The children should be led to sense the difference in mood and to notice the *la* ending where all previous note-song material has ended on *do*.

One way to help children hear the difference between the *la*-centered and *do*-centered songs is through chording. Divide the class into three groups. First, have them sing a *do-mi-so* chord, one group entering at a time, following the teacher's hand sign. Then sing a *la-do-mi* chord, beginning on the same pitch. Without understanding the construction of a major or minor chord, the children will nevertheless hear the difference in the two chords, and if their attention is directed to each note in turn, they may realize that the middle note (the third of the triad) is lower in the *la*-centered chord. When they have reached this point, the term "minor" can be introduced and will have meaning.

It is interesting to note that the terms "major" and "minor" are not used in Hungary with respect to intervals. Rather, they use "nagy" (big) for major and "kicsi" (little) for minor. How much more descriptive these words actually are to children than our words "major" and "minor" which have little meaning outside their musical context.

Once the relative position of *la,* has been established as:

On the line below *do* when *do* is on a line,

In the space below *do* when *do* is in a space,

the children easily derive that low *so* is in the staff position immediately below low *la*. It is easiest to introduce low *so* through a song containing both the low *la* and the low *so,* so that children may discover the *so* from its position below *la,*. An example of a *l,-s,* song is the sea chantey "I've Been to Haarlem":

The strong *do-la,-so,* motif in the first two measures and an uncompli-cated rhythm make this pentatonic song a good choice. There are many examples of *do-la,-so,* and *so,-la,-do* patterns in American folk music. Many more pentatonic American folk songs seem to be built around the scale from low *so* to *mi* or from low *so* to high *la* than have the *do* to *do'* ambit.

After the children can work easily with songs containing low *so* and low *la,* songs with only the low *so* may be examined. For practicing low *so* in a song without low *la,* an easy song example is "Hush, Little Baby." Each new phrase starts with low *so:*

Both the *so,-mi* and *so,-re* intervals exist in this song, and because of its many verses there is ample opportunity for practice on both inter-vals.

For the *so,-do* interval the verse of "Goodbye, Old Paint" uses *so,* as the upbeat leading to *do* for each verse. The hand sign for low *so* is as for *so,* only in the position below low *la:*

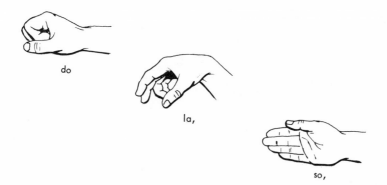

Notes below *do* are indicated in writing with a subprime, for example: low *la* = *l,,* low *so* = *s,.*

With a sight-singing vocabulary extending from low *so* to high *la* there are literally hundreds of pentatonic songs easily available from which to choose the children's singing material. Many can be found right in the school song series. These use folk music extensively and, of the folk music, most of it is pentatonic. The teacher should carefully preview each song to determine whether all of it is within the learned abilities of the children, rhythmically and melodically. Even in instances where a problem exists with part of a song, it can often be used if the teacher gives the difficult section by rote. Usually there is some part of the song that is easily within the reading vocabulary of children in third grade. For the music teacher willing to turn to folk music collections for her song material, there is a vast number of published collections, many specifically aimed at children.

High *do* (*d'*) may be introduced through the cumulative song "Had Me a Bird":

d'	*d'*	*d'*	*s*	*s*	*s*	*d'*	*d'*	*s*
Had	me	a	bird	and	the	bird	pleased	me.

The ambit of this pentatonic song is *do* to high *do,* and its rhythms are simple.

High *do* is not so much a new note as an old friend in a new placement. The hand sign is the same, simply raised to a position above *la:*

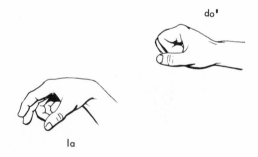

As with each new tone, the children should sing the *d'* in the context of familiar songs, making the new hand sign. They should then see it on the staff, draw it on staff paper in melodic dictation, and, last, recognize it in a new song.

The octaves *re* (*r'*) and *mi* (*m'*) can be taught almost incidentally as they occur in song material. Once sure of the place of high *do*, children have no difficulty recognizing, singing, or placing the high *re* and *mi*. One good song example for deriving both of these notes is the verse of the Southern folk song *Run, Chillun, Run:*

d'	d'	d'	d'	m'	r'	d'	m'	r'	d'	s	l	s	s
That	child	run	and	that	child	flew,	That	child	lost	his	Sun-	day	shoe.

Whenever a new pentatonic song is sung the notes needed should be placed on the chalkboard, either on the staff (as for "Old Blue"):

or as a tonal ladder (as for "Swing Low, Sweet Chariot"):

l

s

m

r

d

l,

s,

Only those notes actually needed for the song should be placed on the chalkboard. When constructing a tonal ladder care should be taken that space is left where the step and a half occurs (where the *fa* and *ti* are missing).

It is a very graphic aid to young children to have them "be" the notes of the tonal ladder. The larger children should represent the lower notes, and, as the "notes" ascend in pitch, the children should be smaller.* In this way the concept of high and low is correctly reinforced.

---

* This conceptualization of pitch may be compared with the pitch-size relationship existing in resonator bells and in organ pipes.

d   r   m   s   l

Now with the full pentaton in the children's singing vocabulary, the Kodály Book *333 Elementary Exercises in Sight-Singing* may be a useful addition to the lesson, since it provides exercise on tonal patterns not as commonly encountered in song material and yet with which the children must be fluent if they are to progress easily to the next steps in the sequence. In choosing an exercise the teacher should be sure of its pertinence to the specific lesson being taught. For example, if the children have had difficulty with *re-la,* there are specific examples for reinforcing this interval.

There are numerous techniques for making these essentially exercise-like compositions more interesting. They may be sung or clapped in canon, sung as question and answer by pairs of children, or sung by the group against a simple rhythm ostinato. For third grade, however, they should be used sparingly, and only when specifically useful to the learning of a skill which needs additional reinforcement.

Some of these tunes will be familiar to the children if the Kodály Nursery Songs were used in second grade. When asked to compose his Nursery Book, Kodály simply chose from his "333" those that seemed most appropriate, and to these a Hungarian poet contributed the words.

Although the melodic skill teaching material for third grade should be pentatonic, other song material must be taught as well. It takes some time to teach children to sing *mi-fa* and *ti-do* half steps in tune. A certain amount of rote song material for the grade must include these intervals in preparation for their introduction on the conscious level in fourth grade; indeed, the *fa* and *ti* will have occurred in pentachordal and hexachordal rote material since first grade.

Singing should also include increasing numbers of songs with melodic ostinati and descants and should also include rounds and canons. Children may create their own ostinati and descants.

The two notes *so-mi* in varying rhythms may be sung effectively against any *do*-pentaton song. By experimenting, children will discover other pleasing combinations. A simple ascending and descending pentatonic scale descant may be used in the same manner, as for example, with "Cotton-Eyed Joe":

Melodic canon singing may be introduced through rhythm canons. When the children are repeating four-measure rhythms well, the teacher should place one from a familiar song on the chalkboard and ask the children to clap it. When they have clapped it once through correctly, she should ask them to repeat it. This time she should tap the same exercise one measure behind in round style. When the exercise is completed, she should ask the children to describe what she did. The words "round" and "canon" may then be introduced, and the class may divide into sections to read the exercise in canon style. Line drawings on the chalkboard exercise may help children know when to start:

After the children are proficient in rhythm canons, melodic canon may be introduced in the same way, the teacher singing softly in canon after the children in a familiar song. The song need not be designated a round or canon. Most pentatonic songs lend themselves to canon singing.

As at every grade level care must be taken that children are singing correctly, in tune, and with good tone quality. It is important that each music period end with good singing rather than with skill teaching, music writing, or some other activity less likely to encourage a love of music in the young child. The basis of the music program is singing, and the music period should begin and end with a song musically performed.

chapter 8

Kodály for American Schools: Grade Four

Fa and *ti* may be introduced in grade four melodic learning, completing the tones making up the major and minor diatonic scales. The concepts of keys and key signatures will be a large part of the year's work. Key signatures for F, G, D, and B♭ should be introduced, and if the children's prior reading has been restricted to F, G, and C and their related minors, it should now be expanded to include D and B♭ major and their related minors, B and G. Use of absolute note names may be included in reading if teaching time allows.

The rhythmic material for the grade consists of dotted rhythms ♩. ♪ and ♪♩. in the familiar duple and triple meters and of the introduction of compound meter. Early in the year the dotted rhythms may be introduced. Children will remember from second and third grade work that the dot is equal to a tied note of shorter value (♩. = ♩♩). Perhaps in fourth grade, where children have a more complete concept of fractions and fractional parts, it will be possible to draw from them the fact that the dot is equal to half the value of the note it follows. Using the example of ♩♩ and ♩. , the children can see that the dot is equal to the one-beat "ta," or half the time value of the two-beat "ta." This understanding should come from singing and hearing while tapping the beat, not simply from seeing notes on the chalkboard.

The dotted quarter and eighth may be taught as the previous dotted rhythms were:

1. Sung in familiar rote songs,
2. Isolated and clapped,

3. Placed on the chalkboard
   first as straight rhythm patterns,

then with ties,

and then with the dot,

In the tied and dotted rhythms the duration syllables simply omit the middle t—ta-i ti instead of ta ti ti. The dotted quarter and eighth note pattern occurs in each phrase of the Southern plantation song "Run, Children Run":

The eighth-dotted quarter note pattern should be shown on the chalkboard first as the syncopation pattern the children already know:

Then it may be shown with the tie,

and last, with the dot,

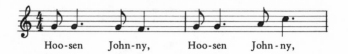

ti   ta - i

This pattern, although not common in American folk music, is repeated in the refrain of the Illinois folk song "Hoosen Johnny":

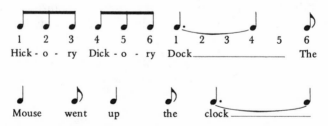

Hoo-sen   John-ny,   Hoo-sen   John-ny,

Songs in which these dotted rhythms occur may be sung with the rhythm duration syllables added as another verse. Then the rhythm should be found in other known songs and their patterns derived by teacher and class together a phrase at a time.

Compound meter, while among the most natural for American children to sing or to respond to rhythmically with skipping, swaying, etc., can sometimes be difficult for them to grasp as a conscious learning. It is absolutely essential that both duple and triple meter be thoroughly understood and that this understanding be behaviorally observable before $\frac{6}{8}$ is introduced. Only when operating with complete ease in these two meters can a child hope to grasp the more complicated metric form of compound meters.

It is sometimes helpful to return to nursery rhymes for the initial lesson since most of our English-language nursery rhymes are in $\frac{6}{8}$ meter:

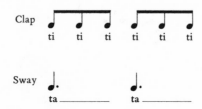

The class may say the familiar rhyme, clapping the threes while swaying to the larger feeling of the twos:

Clap
ti   ti   ti   ti   ti   ti

Sway
ta _____   ta _____

The rhythm of the rhyme should be notated on the board at this point and the children led to see and hear that they are clapping ti, the eighth note, as the beat. Up to this time ta, the quarter note, has always been the beat note in songs used for rhythm reading.

The cowboy song "Go Slow, Little Dogies" is a good one for initial teaching of $\frac{6}{8}$. It holds no tonal difficulties, being pentatonic, and it includes only the most common $\frac{6}{8}$ rhythm patterns: ♫♪ ♫♪ and ♩ ♪♩ ♪ .

Go   slow   lit - tle   dog - ies,   stop   mil - ing   a - round,

The Christmas carol "Joseph Dearest, Joseph Mild" is particularly useful for the quarter-eighth repeated pattern, and also, incidentally, excellent later on for reinforcing the note *fa:*

$\frac{6}{8}$ ♩   ♪ ♩   ♪ | ♩   ♪ ♩. |

    s   m   d   m   s   l   s

Jo - seph dear - est,   Jo - seph mild,

The ♩ ♪♩ ♪ rhythm is one American children have skipped to from early childhood. If $\frac{6}{8}$ rote material has been included as suggested at each grade level, with children encouraged to respond by skipping and clapping the rhythm, these rote songs may now be returned to and their rhythm patterns notated and analyzed.

So that children will not equate compound meter with only $\frac{6}{8}$ it is good to introduce some other examples as well. The $\frac{9}{8}$ folk song "Down In the Valley" is one in which the nine small beats and the three large ones are easily felt:

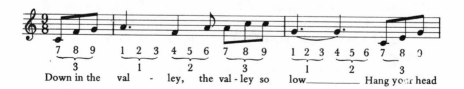

7 8 9   1 2 3   4 5 6   7 8 9   1 2 3   4 5 6   7 8 9

    3   1   2   3   1   2   3

Down in the   val -   ley,   the val - ley so   low_____ Hang your head

The lower part (8) of the meter sign may be taught as representing one *ti* in all songs where the eighth note is the beat note.

If time allows, the terms "quarter note," "eighth note," "half note," and "whole note" may be introduced and used interchangeably with the rhythm duration syllables in discussions about rhythm. However, the rhythm duration syllables will still be used for actual rhythm reading.

The scale tones *fa* and *ti* are the new tonal learnings for grade four. *Fa* should be introduced first. Many of the rote songs of grade three will have included the *fa*. From these, several should be selected which have the repeated *fa* in a strong position. For example, "Joseph Dearest, Joseph Mild," (third line):

or "New River Train" (third line):

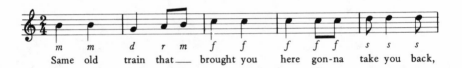

Perhaps one of the best songs for initial teaching of *fa* is the American folk song "Juba" which contains only the notes *so, fa, mi, re,* and *do,* and has *fa* in every phrase:

Several teaching periods should be spent working on familiar rote songs including the *fa* before it is made conscious. Particular attention should be paid to in-tune singing of the *mi-fa* half step and to making children feel the smallness of the interval.

The initial lesson in which children see *fa* in staff notation should be in the key of C or G so that no key signature will be necessary. Using the song "Look Who Is Here, Punchinello, Funny Fellow," the steps might be as follows:

1. Teacher and children derive the *known sol-fa* notation on the chalkboard in contour notation, singing "hmm" for the unknown note:

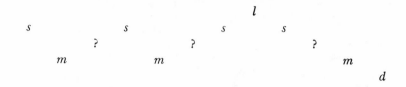

2. Teacher then gives the hand sign for the new note. Class sings, again using "hmm" but with the correct hand sign.
3. Teacher sings the song through in *sol-fa* using the new syllable *fa*.
4. Class sings the song using the new syllable *fa*.

The lesson should be followed up by the children's writing the song in G-*do* staff notation, the *fa* in red for emphasis. As a guide, the teacher may place on the chalkboard:

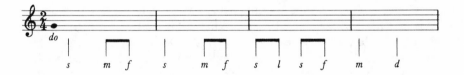

The same exercise should then be written in C-*do*. A child might give placement of the first three notes on the board to help the class get started. At the end of the writing period the entire song should be placed in staff notation on the chalkboard so that there is immediate correction of any mistake.

In a subsequent lesson, after children are singing, reading, and writing *fa* easily in C- and G-*do*, it will be time to introduce the meaning of the one-flat key signature necessary for *fa* in F-*do*. In order to do this, have the children first sing a song with the descending line *so-fa-mi-re-do* in G-*do*. Example: "Whistle, Daughter, Whistle":

Construct a scale of children in front of the class, being sure that the children representing *mi* and *fa* stand close together:

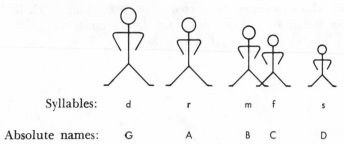

Syllables: d   r   m   f   s

Absolute names: G   A   B   C   D

Have the class sing the song with syllables while the teacher touches each child at those points in the song where his note occurs. The teacher is "playing" the song on the child-scale. Then have the children sing the absolute note names for each child in the scale, calling *do* G. The song should be sung again, this time with absolute note names as the teacher taps the child representing each note. If the class can do this with ease, it is time to introduce the concept of the function of sharps and flats in key signature.

While the child-scale is standing, the teacher may suggest singing the song in F-*do*, and ask the children, "What additional note will we need?" Another child will have to join the child-scale to be F. The class will probably realize that for this song in F the note D will not be needed, so that child may sit down. It is important that none of the other children have changed their positions. The scale will look like this:

F   G   A   B   C

The children should then sing the F-scale with *sol-fa* names and the teacher ask, "What is wrong with our scale?"

The children, who have been taught to expect the small step between *mi* and *fa,* will see that it is now between *fa* and *so.* Reverting to absolute names, the teacher may ask, "What must we do with B if it is too close to C?" The children will suggest moving the B closer to A. The teacher may then say, "When we move a note down to make it closer to the note below it, we must use this sign, '♭,' in front of it and we call this new note 'flat.' " Our note is B. To make it fit the F-scale and sound right, we must make it B-flat (B♭)."

The song should then be sung in absolute names in F, substituting B-flat for B. It is unfortunate that we must use a two-syllable sound, "B-flat," here on one note, but in the English language we have no correct alternative choice. In Hungary there are one-syllable names for all sharped and flatted note; e.g., B♭ is written as "Bé," pronounced "bay," and F♯ is written as "Fisz," pronounced "feese."

At the children's first writing of *fa* in F-*do* they should place the flat before each B as it occurs in the song. This will help to reinforce their understanding of the actual function of the flat in key signature. After this they may look at song examples in books and discover that the sign for the flat need occur only at the beginning of each staff, on the B-line, in order to apply to all the Bs in the song, and that it will always indicate that the song is in F-*do*.

Ti is best introduced through a minor pentachordal song, since it is rarely in a melodically important position in major diatonic songs. Few American folk songs use *ti* as more than a passing tone, so perhaps it would be better to use a good composed song, such as Praetorius' "Rise Up, O Flame":

or a foreign folk song, such as the Russian one, "The Birch Tree":

The procedure is much the same as for introducing *fa*. Many songs with *ti* should be sung by rote. The hand sign may be given and the position of *ti* between *do* and low *la*. Example: "The Birch Tree":

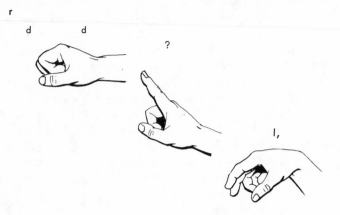

The hand sign for *ti* points up toward *do,* indicating the smallness of the step between the two notes. The unknown note is first hummed in the song, the rest of which is sung in *sol-fa* and with hand signs. Then the teacher sings the song in *sol-fa,* supplying the new note. The song may then be written on the staff by the children in either F-*do* or C-*do* without any difficulty.

When the *ti* is easily sung, recognized, and written in F- and C-*do,* it is time to introduce the concept of sharp in key signature. Again a child-scale should be constructed, this time from the F-*do* minor penta-chord:

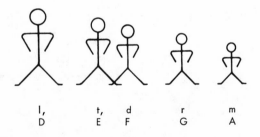

In this case the *ti* and *do* must stand close together to emphasize the smallness of that interval. The terms "whole step" and "half step" can be introduced at this time and related to the child-scale.

The song should be sung in *sol-fa* and in absolute note names as the teacher taps, in song order, the children representing each note. After singing the absolute note names in F, the teacher may ask the class,

"What must we do to make these notes fit G-*do?*" The children will see that the fourth child, G, is now *do* and that this new *do* and the new *ti* (the third child) are no longer close together, as they must be. The new *ti* must be moved "up" until it is again close to the new *do:*

F-*do*	minor	*l,*		*t, d*	*r*	*m*
	pentachord	D		E F	G	A
G-*do*	change to minor	*l,*	*t,*	*d*	*r*	*m*
	pentachord	E	F	G	A	B

The teacher must then explain that to make the F move up we must put a sharp sign "♯" in front of it and change its absolute name to F-sharp. The class should then sing the song again in absolute note names in G-*do,* using the name F-sharp where it occurs.

Initially in the music writing of *ti* in G-*do* the sharp should be shown in the first space, where children sing it. Children may then be told that the one-sharp key signature always means G-*do.* In the lessons that follow, children can be shown that in printed music the one sharp is usually placed on the fifth line of the staff, rather than in the first space. If they understand that the one sharp in the key signature means that F is always sharped wherever it occurs in the song, the more usual key signature will present little added difficulty.

The keys of D and B♭ major and their related minors may be introduced in much the same way. As scale patterns become firmly learned it may not be necessary to use children as scale steps. However, the more concrete the beginning steps, the better able the children will be to cope with more abstract learnings at later stages.

In singing, the fourth-grade class should be facile with rounds and canons and should be beginning two-part work. The small volume of two-part songs, *Bicinia Hungarica I,* is an excellent choice for starting on part singing, as are some of the easier selections in the Julliard Repertory Library. Attention must be given, as always, to singing with artistry. Dynamics and tone quality should be stressed in each lesson. Children should be encouraged to feel the beauty of the music they make, not simply to understand the mechanics of it.

chapter 9

Kodály for American Schools: Grades Five and Six

Fifth and sixth grades are years of practice and of putting to use the skill and concept learnings of the first four grades. There is further material to be learned, but the foundation of music literacy has by now been laid, and the primary work of the last two elementary years should be the securing and the reinforcing of this literacy. The known skills and concepts must now be applied to increasingly sophisticated song material, including that of well-known composers. Part-singing should occupy a portion of every lesson. In both grades, however, about 50 percent of the new music should be taught by a rote or rote-note process to ensure continued high interest on the part of the children.

Grade Five

The new material for the grade includes, in rhythm, common time and cut time; triplets ⎣⎯⎯⎦ and ⎣⎯⎯⎦ ; dotted eight-note and sixteenth-note combinations ▆ (timri) and ▆ (tir-rim); the less common meters $\frac{2}{8}$, $\frac{3}{8}$, $\frac{4}{8}$, and $\frac{5}{8}$; and songs of mixed meter. Melodic learning should include classification of songs, by sight and sound, as belonging to major and minor scales; scale construction; major and minor interval identification; the Aeolian, Dorian, and Mixolydian modes; the natural ♮ and accidentals of the sharped *fa* (*fi*) and flatted *ti* (*ta*), necessary for the modal scales; and the sharped *so* (*si*), needed for melodic minor. There should be some diagramming of song form and creation of simple melodies within known scales and forms. If absolute note names were introduced in grade three and reinforced in grade four, reading and

100

writing in absolute notes should be expanded now to include the keys of E♭ and A♭ and their related minors.

Rhythmic Learning for Grade Five

In order to teach cut time (*alla breve*) to children it is necessary that they first be familiar with the symbol for $\frac{4}{4}$, common time ("C"). This may usually be found in school series music books, frequently in marches. The children can derive the meaning of the "C" simply by counting the beats in a measure, and discover that "C" is another way of writing $\frac{4}{4}$. While it would be possible simply to tell children that the "C" with a line through it means $\frac{2}{2}$—two beats in a measure and a half note equal to one beat—it would certainly be more meaningful to have them sing a cut-time song by rote, feeling the two beats per measure and then to look at the song in their books and find the signature "¢." Knowing that they have been counting only two beats to a measure, they should be able to deduce that the numerical signature would be $\frac{2}{2}$. They will see and hear in their own singing that cut-time is simply a speeded-up $\frac{4}{4}$.

The dotted eighth followed by a sixteenth note, ⌐▪ ▪, is fairly common in American folk music, while the sixteenth followed by a dotted eighth note, ▪⌐. , is common in Hungary and comparatively rare here. Both should be learned from song material, and shown first as tied notes:

The traditional Southern song "Marching Down the Levee" is a possible one for introducing the dotted-eight-sixteenth pattern:

We're march-in' down the lev - ee,   We're march-in' down the   lev - ee,

The Texas folk song "Rain, Come Wet Me" has the less common six-teenth-dotted-eighth pattern four times:

Rain,   come   wet____ me,   Sun,   come   dry____ me

Triplets, , are called tri-o-la in rhythm duration syllables. They are somewhat uncommon in folk music but do occasionally occur, as in the spiritual "Lonesome Valley":

No - bod - y else_____ could walk it   for Him

The less common meters, $\frac{3}{8}$, $\frac{9}{8}$, $\frac{12}{8}$, will more often be found in composed than in folk material. It is important to teach children how to derive the meter of an unfamiliar song. If they are sure in the basic meters, $\frac{2}{4}$, $\frac{3}{4}$, $\frac{4}{4}$ and $\frac{6}{8}$, they should not encounter difficulty with odd meters or with heterometric song material.

Some possible choices for teaching the less common meters are as follows: for $\frac{3}{8}$, "Barnyard Song" by Edvard Grieg:

The__ barn door's now   o - pen, Come__ out friend-ly   cow

for $\frac{9}{8}$, the French-Canadian folk song "The Canadian":

Down where the riv - er flows, where the tall pine tree grows

and for $\frac{12}{8}$, "He Shall Feed His Flock":

He ____ shall feed his flock like a shep ____ herd

To help children cope with more than one meter in a song, a simple beginning heterometric song is "Coffee Grows on White Oak Trees," in which the verse is in triple and the chorus in duple meter. A more metrically complicated song, "Shenandoah," has meter shifts in every phrase, but because of its melodic unity, is not difficult for children.

Melodic Learning for Grade Five

Since the introduction of *la* in grade three, children have been aware of *do*-ending or major mode songs and of *la*-ending or minor mode songs. With the introduction of key signatures in grade four and the associated scale-construction activities, the half step and whole step concept was introduced. In fifth grade this knowledge should be applied to all music-reading material. Children should, by looking at the key signature and the final note of a new song, be able to determine whether it is *do*- or *la*-centered and, by looking through the song, what its scale is. This scale should then be placed on the chalkboard and practiced with hand-singing before the song is read. Children should be given time to read any new song silently before being asked to sing at sight.

When the construction of basic major and minor scales holds no difficulty for the children, it is time to introduce the alterations that produce other scales. Basic whole-step-half-step patterns of the major and the minor scales are

major:	1	2	3⌣4	5	6	7 8	
	d	*r*	*m f*	*s*	*l*	*t d*	
			½			½	
minor:	1	2⌣3	4	5⌣6	7	8	
	l,	*t, d*	*r*	*m f*	*s*	*l*	
		½		½			

By starting at any point in the *sol-fa* scale, it is possible to sing a modal scale simply by singing up eight steps, being careful to maintain the half-steps between *mi* and *fa* and between *ti* and *do:*

do	to	*do'*	—	Ionian Mode
re	to	*re'*	—	Dorian Mode
mi	to	*mi'*	—	Phrygian Mode
fa	to	*fa'*	—	Lydian Mode
so	to	*so'*	—	Mixolydian Mode
la	to	*la'*	—	Aeolian Mode

(The scale on *ti* is never used.)

The scale on *fa* is so rare in folk music of the Western world as to be of only academic interest, and the scale on *mi* also is uncommon. Modal American folk music tends to be Ionian (what we think of simply as "major"), Aeolian (what we think of as "pure minor"), Dorian, or Mixolydian; so that for practical purposes only two new modal scales need really be made familiar to children—the Dorian and the Mixolydian. However, it is sometimes easier for children to understand the construction of these two scales in the context of all modal scales.

Modal scales may be classified broadly as being either major or minor in character, depending upon whether the interval from the first to the third step of the scale is a major or a minor one. By considering all minor modes as *la*-centered and all major ones as *do*-centered, the alterations necessary to produce each mode become quickly apparent and form a pattern easy to remember:

Major Modes

IONIAN (our "major" scale):   *d   r   m f   s   l   t d*

LYDIAN (the scale on *fa*):   *d   r   m   fi s   l   t d* (sharped *fa*)

MIXOLYDIAN (the scale on *so*): *d   r   m f   s   l ta   d* (flatted *ti*)

Minor Modes

AEOLIAN ("pure minor"):   *l,   t, d   r   m f   s   l*

DORIAN (the scale on *re*): *l,   t, d   r   m f fi s   l* (sharped *fa*)

PHRYGIAN (the scale on *mi*): *l, ta,   d   r   m f   s   l* (flatted *ti*)

Essentially this means that by simply being able to 1) hear whether a scale is major or minor in character, and 2) hear the altered *fa* or *ti,* we can classify any song by mode.

A well-known American folk song in Mixolydian mode is "Old Joe Clark." The major-mode feeling of the song is unmistakable, and the flatted *ti* occurs repeatedly. Notice the strong major feeling of the chorus,

Round and round,   old Joe Clark

and the repeatedly flatted seventh of the verse:

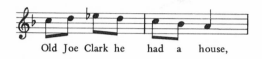

Old Joe Clark he   had   a   house,

The second phrase of the Newfoundland folk song "As I Roved Out," with its raised *fa,* is an example of the Dorian mode:

As   I   roved   out   one   fine   sum-mer's eve - nin'

To   view   the   flow'rs   and   to   take   the —— air,

To simplify the entire thing for children:

The *la* scale + *fi* = Dorian Mode.
The *do* scale + *ta* = Mixolydian Mode.

They will have little immediate need for the other modes.

There is one other scale alteration children should be taught at this time: the sharped *so—si.* This is necessary for reading in melodic or harmonic minor. The hand signs for the three scale alterations to be taught in fifth grade are

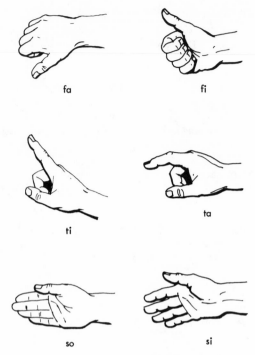

fa

fi

ti

ta

so

si

(open fingers and raise hand slightly)

Again in fifth grade much time should be spent in producing beautiful singing. More music of the great composers should be brought into the song repertory, and interpretation emphasized. Hopefully there will be time in the schedule for choir involvement for fifth-grade children. The experience of working for a longer time on a few pieces of good music to polish them for performance is a good one for children, as long as it does not take time away from the instructional music program.

Grade Six

The new material for the grade will include singing intervals with their inversions, the concept of the triad, identification and singing of broken chords and triads, rhythmic diminution and augmentation, and reading and writing the F and C clefs. In addition, there should be further study of musical form and continued work on major, minor, and modal scales.

The song material used for teaching these new skills and concepts may include more good composed music, although many new songs will still probably be from folk music literature. Good examples of both folk and composed song material are available in fifth- and sixth-grade song books of most basic series as well as in the Julliard Repertory Library, now available for school use.

Rhythmic Learning for Grade Six

As with all musical skills, augmentation and diminution are taught best through singing and hearing, deriving the visual symbols as an end step. They present little difficulty for children if taught through a well-known simple song such as the French round "Brother John." With the notation on the chalkboard, the class sings the round in the familiar way first. Then the teacher may ask, "How can we change this to make it more interesting?" Children will come up with many possible changes, but usually among the first things suggested is "faster" or "slower." Whichever is mentioned first, the class should perform the song in that way and then derive the notation for the "new" way on the chalkboard. Once the "old" way and the "new" way are on the board, the class may try singing one against the other. If they have chosen to do the song faster first, they will see that by doing it slower they can add still a different dimension. The words "diminution" and "augmentation" may be introduced as they apply to rhythm, and the children should then try writing augmented and diminished rhythms to other easy familiar songs.

Example: "Brother John":

Normal:

Diminished:

Augmented:

Melodic and Harmonic Learning for Grade Six

Children should have been singing intervals as a part of their regular music lesson for some time now. Hopefully they have been singing the size of the interval as well as its syllables.

Example:

In sixth grade these known intervals may be placed on the chalkboard with their inversions as they are sung:

	Interval			Its Inversion
m-d	major third		m-d'	minor sixth
s-d	perfect fifth		s-d'	perfect fourth
r-d	major second		r-d'	minor seventh
f-d	perfect fourth		f-d'	perfect fifth
s-m	minor third		s-m'	major sixth

From this systematization of intervals and their inversions, children should be able to deduce the rules:

1. The inversion of a major interval is always minor.
2. The inversion of a perfect interval is always perfect.

Once the children have reached an understanding of major, minor, and perfect intervals they should start to categorize all scale intervals in this fashion, adding to individual lists in their notebooks as they find the intervals in their songs and exercises.

Seconds		Thirds		Fourths		Fifths	
Major	Minor	Major	Minor	Perfect	Augmented	Perfect	Diminished
d-r	m-f	d-m	r-f	d-f	f-t	d-s	t-f
r-m	t-d	f-l	m-s	r-s	[all whole	r-l	[contains
f-s		s-t	l-d	m-l	steps = an	m-t	2 half
s-l			t-r	s-d	augmented	f-d	steps]
l-t				l-r	fourth]	s-r	
				t-m		l-m	

The sixths are simply inversions of the thirds; the sevenths, of the seconds.

The concept of the triad has been touched on earlier. Even in third and fourth grade there was probably some chord singing. In sixth grade basic harmony may be begun by applying chording to scale steps and using the tonic, dominant, and subdominant chords in vocal accompaniments to song material.

Basically a simple chord is the first, third, and fifth built on any note in the scale of the song being considered. The tonic, built on the first step of the scale (*do* in major, *la* in minor), and the dominant, built on the fifth step of the scale (*so* in major, *mi* in minor), should be taught first since they are the two most common chords in music. Many songs need only these two chords for an artistic harmonic accompaniment.

Example: "Skip to My Lou":

Inversions of these chords should be taught before going on to other chords. They will facilitate chordal accompaniment singing. The possible inversions are:

		m				*t*
	d	*d*			*s*	*s*
s	*s*	*s*		*r*	*r*	*r*
m	*m*			*t*	*t*	
d				*s*		
root position	first inversion	second inversion		root position	first inversion	second inversion
	I Chord				*V Chord*	

Starting from the I chord in its root position, the class should decide which inversion of the V chord is easiest to sing:

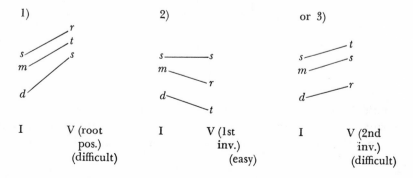

The children see that the first inversion leads most comfortably to and from the tonic chord. They should then practice three-part chord singing from I to V to I until it is easy for them:

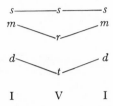

I   V   I

The parts should be shifted around the class so that all children have practice with the upper, middle, and lower voices. One good musical example for practice in chording is the hymn from the Beethoven *Ninth Symphony*. The children can chord at the end of each musical phrase, using only the tonic and dominant chords. This rhythm, with English words, may be found in many of the current music series.

After the class can sing such chordal accompaniments using the I and V chords, the IV chord may be introduced. Again the class should sing the chord with its inversions and decide which inversion moves most smoothly from the tonic and to the dominant. The progression will be

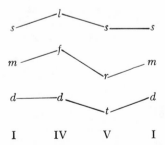

I   IV   V   I

With these three chords a very pleasant accompaniment may be sung to many of the songs the children know. The Mozart *Alleluia* is an example of one that particularly lends itself to this kind of chording.

Triads should of course be practiced in minor as well as major. The same procedure should be used in introducing the basic chords and their inversions, and the progression from I to IV to V and back to I will have to be practiced. Minor chord progression for singing:

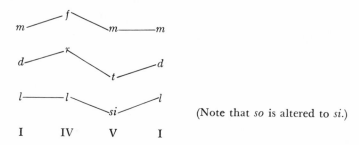

(Note that *so* is altered to *si*.)

It is good, toward the end of sixth grade, to introduce reading in clefs other than the G-clef. Boys' voices will be changing soon, if they have not already, and by the end of junior high school most of their music will be shown in F-clef. Changing clefs will hold no difficulty for children who sing easily in relative *sol-fa*. However, if absolute note names have been taught, they too should be practiced in F- and C-clefs. Each should be introduced through a song already known well in *sol-fa* in G-clef, for example, "Row, Row, Row Your Boat":

Just as the curl of the G-clef is around the line of G in the treble clef, two dots surround the F in the F-clef, and the inward curve of the clef sign shows the third line to be the C in the C-clef. For children facile with *sol-fa,* clef reading will be easy. Once the clefs have been introduced, some of the more familiar songs should be written by the children in the new clefs.

Perhaps the most important work of the sixth grade, however, is the singing of the children. If none of the other suggested sixth-grade material is covered, the loss will not be great if the time has been spent instead on singing, not just the folk songs but now also the beautiful art songs and music composed specifically for young voices to sing in two and three parts. The *Bicinia Hungarica* and *Children's Chorus Music* of Kodály offer a wealth of such music. In addition, there are a number of Béla Bartók songs for treble voices and some American folk songs in beautiful settings by Aaron Copland. Some of the two-part songs of Bach are within the ability range of youngsters with five years of Kodály Method training, as are songs by Mozart, Haydn, Beethoven, and Schubert.

The artistic performance of such music is the most important work of sixth grade. Children who experience the joy of singing beautiful music in two or three voices will surely develop a love of music which will endure throughout their lives.

chapter 10

Problems in Incorporating the Kodály Method in American Systems of Education

The Kodály Method is being used today in the United States with success in a number of schools and school systems. The educational concepts of Kodály were first brought to light in the United States through the writings of Mary Helen Richards, whose *Threshold to Music* books and charts, if somewhat superficial in their presentation of the Method, nevertheless were responsible to a large extent for the present widespread acquaintance with some aspects of the Method. The participation of Kodály himslf and of Erzsébet Szönyi, at the I.S.M.E. Conference at Interlochen, Michigan, and at a subsequent symposium at Stanford University in 1966, contributed further to the development of the Method in this country.

Since that time some problems have emerged in the use of the Method which seem peculiar to our American systems of education. Some of these are general to all music education in the United States, while others are more specific to the use of the Kodály Method in American schools.

It is necessary to understand these problems to use the Kodály Method effectively within American music education systems. In most cases they are quite outside the experience of Hungarian music educators, and so can be solved, if at all, only by experienced American music educators knowledgeable about both the Hungarian method and American schools. The problems may be classified broadly as deriving from four basic areas:

1. The nature of our American culture,
2. School organization and teaching practices,
3. Teacher training,
4. Materials.

The Nature of Our American Culture

The first major problem encountered by any teacher wishing to use the Kodály Method as her basis for instruction is inherent in the American culture itself, if such a term may be used to cover the diverse society of the American people. The school containing Blacks, Puerto Ricans, Orientals, white Anglo-Saxon Protestants, Jews, and Catholics may not be common, but its does exist in some large urban areas, and it offers an intensified version of a problem that exists to some extent in most American schools. What is the common cultural background of American school children? Each group has its own culture, often a rich one, but how is it possible to find a common cultural basis for teaching such a class? In Hungary the homogeneity of the population and its ancient cultural heritage are taken for granted.

In the United States the heterogeneity of population is a problem not just to teachers wishing to use the Kodály Method, but to all educators. It would seem that a possible solution might be for the school to draw on the rich multicultural background of its pupils in devising curriculum and selecting materials. The Kodály Method, with its folk song orientation, seems well designed to help children develop a sense of pride in their diverse cultural heritage, as well as to provide a common and more assimilated American song heritage for them all. Song material can be drawn both from music specific to each cultural group represented in the class and from those folk songs which are more generally American by reason of years of assimilation.

A song of the pre-Civil War period describing the slave escape route—"Follow the Drinking Gourd"—or a song of the Irish-American immigrants building the first transcontinental railway—"Paddy Works on the Railway"—relate to specific groups within our population. Of a more general nature, songs such as "Skip to My Lou" and "Coffee Grows on White Oak Trees," while certainly regional in origin, are not as specific to the history of any one group in the population and may be used to help provide a common culture.

In addition to varied cultural backgrounds there are also students known as "culturally deprived"; this fact raises the question of how to teach a subject built on inherited culture when that culture does not knowingly exist in the background of the children. However, our term "culturally deprived," as it is used educationally in this country, does not necessarily imply *musically* deprived. Noted American anthropologist Carl Withers has reported:

> In the United States [singing games] have lasted better as truly traditional games among less privileged children—for example, in Harlem or in the

Appalachians—than among middle-class children, whose playtime has been almost as completely organized and supervised as their study time.[1]

In other words, it should be even easier to build a singing program on the culture of the so-called culturally deprived than on that of middle-class America, since the singing games to which Withers refers are the earliest music of the Kodály Method.

A very different kind of problem deriving from the nature of American culture is the neglect of music by many school systems concerned with teaching what they consider basic skills—i.e., reading, writing, and arithmetic—to the exclusion of all else. This so-called economy is not practiced only by inner-city schools with genuine budget problems, but also by some of the wealthiest school systems in the United States, under the guise of doing away with "frills." It is very much a part of the American scene to consider the arts as unimportant and unnecessary appendages of education.

There is no simple answer to this problem. Until such time as the American public values music, music will have only a small place in the curriculum. However, it is important to remember that such was also the case in Hungary thirty years ago; the masses in Hungary did not know or value music until recent years. Thus we see that it is possible, through education, to give music a place in the value systems of large numbers of people. Perhaps children in America today, if well educated in music, will not be so quick tomorrow to legislate music out of the curriculum.

In addition to the above-mentioned problems—i.e., the heterogeneous nature of the American school population, the special problems of cultural deprivation, and the common social concept of music as an unimportant frill—there is still another problem characteristic of the American way of life. That is the mobility of the American people. It is not uncommon for an elementary school music teacher in a large urban or suburban school system to face a new child once a week. In a school of 500 children, 100 or more may come and go each school year. Home-selling, "moving up," transfer to another city—these are all aspects of American family life which must realistically be taken into account. A program of music instruction may be sequential to the teacher, but there is nothing sequential about it to the new child entering school in the fourth grade with little or no previous musical experience. Conversely, it can be a depressing experience to the teacher who has worked for five or six years in a school to see her results moving away before she can enjoy them.

[1] Introduction to William Wells Newell, *Games and Songs of American Children* (New York: Dover Publications, Inc., 1963), p. vii.

There is no complete answer to the mobility problem. A teacher cannot keep her children from moving away or new children from moving in. However, she can moderate the effect of this mobility somewhat. In the lower grades children seem able to catch up to some extent to their classmates, particularly if a buddy system is used and a youngster who understands the work well is assigned to sit beside and help the new child. Unfortunately, the child entering at fifth or sixth grade can rarely bridge the gap. If there are ten such children in a class (and this can happen), the problem becomes acute.

A possible solution for the older children would be regrouping across grade lines for instruction in music. In this manner the beginning children in fourth, fifth, and sixth grades could be placed together in one group and the more advanced students could be similarly grouped. In schools with more than one class per grade level, regrouping for music could be even more easily accomplished. This kind of grouping and regrouping has been done in some American schools for many years for reading and mathematics, and in some few schools for music. The only real deterrent is the difficulties such a scheme may cause administrative organization. Regrouping for music depends, in the final analysis, upon whether instruction is to be organized for ease of administration, or whether the function of administration is to provide for effective instruction. If the latter is so, then regrouping for music should meet with no objection, and, to some extent, the problems caused by population mobility can be circumvented.

Another aspect of the American culture which might be considered by some to be a deterrent to the use of the Kodály Method in American schools is the prevalence of the "pop-rock" culture. Many people, among them prominent music educators, maintain that as popular music is the common background of young people it should be used in the curriculum for instructional purposes. However, there has been very little success reported in using such music for teaching the basic skills and concepts of music to children. Youngsters enjoy listening to popular music, dancing to popular music, singing or playing popular music. They do not, as a rule, enjoy analyzing it for melodic contour, form, or chord structure. It is recreational music, and its amusement value tends to lessen as it is used for instructional purposes.

The fact that popular music exists in the culture does not mean that it must be mirrored in the education system. Many things exist in our culture which we do not consider to be of sufficient value to include in the curricula of our schools, particularly at the elementary grade levels.

In Hungary, where music instruction in the lower schools is based entirely on the Kodály Method, there is excellent high school and college level instruction available for those students who wish to pursue the study of popular music. In adulthood such study seems reasonable, but in early childhood it would seem that the function of the school should be to broaden the cultural horizons, not merely to reinforce the limited cultural background from which so many children come.

There are no all-embracing answers to the problems raised by the diversified American culture, i.e., 1) the heterogeneous nature of the American population, 2) cultural deprivation, 3) the social concept of music as an unimportant subject, 4) the mobility of the population, 5) the importance of popular music in America.

Each of these problems will have to be recognized and solved individually, school by school, and teacher by teacher.

School Organization and Teaching Practices

A second major problem area could be considered to lie within school organization in the United States. Traditionally in American schools music has been strongest at the high school level, where a marching band was needed to send off the football team. From the high school level music filtered down to the junior high or middle school, and then, if there was any money left, one or two elementary music teachers were hired to cover all the elementary schools in the district.

In hours per week of music taught by a music specialist, still today the middle and upper schools have far more than the lower schools—in spite of the fact that the junior high school general music class, usually required, offers little but frustration for either pupils or teacher in many instances. It can hardly be otherwise when the children so often come to the junior high level without the most basic skills of music literacy.

In such traditionally organized systems the Kodály Method cannot succeed without first changing the organization. A necessary task of the teacher who wishes to use the method in such a system is to first convince the local board of education to give sufficient time to music education in the elementary grades. The absurdity of beginning a subject from the top down should be obvious. No one would consider scheduling only one half hour a week to reading or mathematics in the primary grades and then increasing the time to four hours a week in high school. Yet this is what happens in most places with music. Tradition and vested interests in maintaining the status quo die hard. It is important to ask not for less music at the upper levels of public education but for enough music at the lower levels to adequately prepare children for more effective instruction at the upper levels.

In some systems the Kodály Method has been introduced at the junior high school level, where the teacher or supervisor has felt the frequency of music instruction would make it feasible. However, aside from the obvious difficulty of interesting fourteen- and fifteen-year-olds in beginning with two- and three-note songs, the development of accurate tonal memory is a slow process and should begin early if it is to be effective. The adolescent may intellectualize more easily, but he generally cannot develop as fine an intervallic tonal memory as he would have developed had his singing and ear training been started at three or six years of age.

Traditional school organizations do not present the only problems to music instruction. School systems getting away from traditional approaches bring, with innovation, new sets of problems. The open-space classroom is a large open area containing two to four teachers and a number of children sufficient to fill two, three, or four classrooms; it is undivided by traditional one teacher-one class lines either in terms of room arrangement or in terms of instruction. Such an arrangement can either foster excellent music instruction or can result in a total loss in the area of music. In a team of four classroom teachers, hopefully, one will be able to carry on music instruction in systems lacking a professional music teacher, or where the music teacher has very limited time with each group. Further, because released time for planning is so essential to classroom teachers working in open space, some systems are providing full-time art, physical education, and music personnel to such schools. The specialists take all the children at the same hour, thus giving the open-space teachers released time for planning and coordination. For the specialist this means freedom to regroup children for effective instruction, and, often, an increase in weekly instructional time. In such a situation the results can be excellent for the music program, and the Kodály Method can be used with a high degree of success.

On the less favorable side, when sufficient specialist time is not provided, the open-space grouping seems to lead in some instances toward ignoring music altogether, as too difficult to handle with a large group, or toward the subservience of music to other subject matter. The latter occurs when music is used as a vehicle to teach other subjects—science, the social sciences, even mathematics—and is not considered a subject in its own right.

This use of music is, of course, not restricted to open-space situations and is not a new one. For years music has been correlated with everything from the study of Indians (where it can be appropriate) to the study of the solar system (where it is not). In almost all such correlation the music is of secondary importance. The skills and concepts taught through the music are not musical ones. Music is a subject with a body of knowledge, i.e., musical concepts and skills. Any use of music which does not increase the student's knowledge of these concepts and skills cannot validly be termed music instruction.

One last problem relating to school organization is that of the changing function of the music specialist. In many systems in the past the elementary school music specialist both taught music classes and guided the elementary classroom teacher in the follow-up of the music lesson. The responsibility for the music program lay between the two teachers— one to give direction, the other to reinforce. Although this arrangement may still be found in some parts of the country, the trend seems to be away from classroom teacher participation in the music program. With teachers' unions and associations becoming more influential, greater pressure is being applied to school systems to provide daily released time to teachers for planning. The function of the music teacher in many such systems has become primarily one of providing this released time for the classroom teacher. In practical terms this can be good, if the time given to the music teacher is two or more lessons a week per class, but, unfortunately, it tends more often to mean no actual increase in instructional time for the music teacher, and a loss of any possible cooperation and follow-up by the classroom teacher. The classroom teacher in many places has been totally withdrawn from responsibility for the music program, without any additional compensatory time being given to the music teacher. State guides may list an hour or ninety minutes a week of music as desirable at the elementary level, but in reality the amount of music taught tends to be more and more dependent upon the specialist hours. Again, without sufficient time allotment the Kodály Method cannot be effectively used.

To recapitulate: The problems relating to school organization and teacher practices are basically:

1. The concentration of music education at the upper school levels in traditional school systems,

2. Innovative educational practices, such as open-space classrooms, which may not always make sufficient provision for music instruction,

3. The use of music as a means to teaching other subjects rather than as a subject in itself,

4. The changing function of the music specialist.

The music teacher can do little except press for change where these situations exist.

Teacher Training

In Hungary, the Franz Liszt Academy of Music in Budapest and its six affiliate institutions in other parts of the country now have teachers trained sufficiently well in the Kodály Method to train student teachers and to retrain practicing teachers. The Method has been in use for many years, and in that time there has been concentrated effort to bring teacher-training in the Method to every corner of Hungary. It was, after all, the area of teacher-training that first interested Kodály. He realized that with inadequately trained teachers, little or nothing could be accomplished.

In the United States today we have the same problem that faced Hungary thirty years ago, with little possibility of a uniform means to its solution. Although requirements vary widely from state to state and from university to university, as a general rule thirty or fewer academic undergraduate credits are sufficient in a student's major field to give him a degree and a teacher's certificate in that field. Thirty college credits in music, in addition to the usual general academic credits for the bachelor's degree, are usually enough to put a student into a school system as a music specialist. In terms of course work, this is less than a year and a half's work if taken consecutively.

The Kodály Method requires thorough musicianship of its practitioners. It is not a series of gimmicks or a get-results-quick approach. In order to be able to use this Method correctly, the teacher using it must have had enough movable-*do* solfege to operate easily with it; thorough knowledge of form and analysis; harmony and ethnomusicology; as well as conducting, voice training, and training in the Method itself.

Few teachers' colleges are giving these kinds of course offerings to their music-education majors, and yet such a background is essential if the Kodály Method is to be used intelligently in this country. In Hungary the teacher-training candidate has to pass the most rigorous entrance examination in the entire advanced music school. His musical proficiency must be greater than that of students majoring in performance or in composition. His program is designed to produce not only a good teacher but also a fine musician. The philosophy of "let him who cannot do, teach" does not apply in Hungarian schools. It does seem to apply at times in America.

There are certainly many fine music schools and departments in the United States, but not enough to produce quality music teachers for all the systems that need them. The problem then is one of making more comprehensive and thorough the music training in institutions which are not primarily music schools, or which do not have large music departments. This in turn can be hastened if school systems will insist upon certain levels of competency from job candidates rather than simply credits on a transcript.

With a good musical background, the teacher-training candidate or the music teacher returning to school for refresher courses can obtain thorough training in the Kodály Method. Such training takes time, thought, and trial and error in the classroom. And it necessitates working with teachers properly trained and qualified in the Kodály Method.

As happens with many new forms of educational thought when they come to the United States, the Kodály Method is ostensibly being practiced far and wide by people who have had little or no real training in it and whose sole knowledge of it comes from commercial materials which in some cases incorporate only the most superficial aspects of the Method—the *sol-fa* syllables and the hand signs. They have seen only the tip of the iceberg and do not even know that the rest of it is there. Quick summer courses, one and two-day workshops, often given by totally uncertified people, add to this morass of bad teaching. One has only to glance through the pages of music journals any spring to see the numerous course offerings in the Kodály Method—far too numerous from the standpoint of quality education.

Where may a teacher properly equip herself in the Method? First and foremost, of course, in Hungary. Every year an ever larger group of international students arrives in Budapest to work for a few months or for a year at the Liszt Academy and in the Singing Schools. A regular program of study has been devised for these people to acquaint them with the Kodály Method at every level and to give them the musical and teaching skills necessary for use of the Method. Those who satisfactorily complete a year or more of such study receive a Certificate from the Academy authorizing them to practice the Method and to teach it to other teachers.

For teachers unable to spend a year in Hungary, courses given in the United States by teachers who have spent such a year and are certified should prove helpful. In addition, not to be overlooked are the fine Hungarian teachers who have come to America. Many of these are thoroughly conversant with the Method. A word of caution here, however. Not all Hungarian musicians are necessarily qualified in the Kodály Method. Some teaching and writing has been done in recent years by Hungarian-Americans totally unqualified in the Method. A twenty-year-old certificate from the Liszt Academy in violin or piano does not indicate a qualified teacher in the Kodály Method. Neither does a past personal friendship with Kodály. The student should assure himself of the qualifications of a teacher before investing in a course.

The student with two years to spend and a desire to have the most complete training possible may wish to apply for admission to the Kodály Institute at Wellesley, Massachusetts, an institution with many fine Hungarian and American teachers on its staff and with close ties with the Liszt Academy. A year in Hungary is part of the two-year program. On the West Coast an advanced degree program with emphasis in Kodály has been offered in Oakland, California, since 1971 at the College of the Holy Names, where the staff includes Liszt Academy-trained Kodály Certificate-holders, both Hungarian and American. As of this writing there is no other Kodály degree program utilizing certified Kodály teachers.

The student is advised most strongly to avoid any courses listed as Kodály-Orff, since such a combination cannot in reality exist. The practitioners of Orff may choose to include *sol-fa* syllables and hand signs in their teaching—they often do—but these are mere externals of the Kodály Method. The whole philosophy of Kodály, that everything *must* begin with singing, precludes absolutely the use of instruments until after the child has the elements of music literacy. This philosophy is obviously incompatible with the practices of the Orff Institute. People knowledgeable in either method do not attempt to combine them.

As more qualified teachers in the Method become available, it is to be hoped that more colleges and universities will offer work in the Method. The careful long-range planning and detailed week-to-week and day-to-day planning required of the teacher working with the Method, the skill and concept orientation of the approach, the behavioristic way of looking at every response, cannot help but influence teaching for the better. This kind of training at the college level could produce better teachers even if they never used the Method as such.

Materials

One might suppose that the differences between Hungarian and American folk songs could cause problems in applying the Hungarian concept and skill sequence to American materials. That there are differences is obvious. The Hungarian infant songs are based on three notes, *so-mi-la,* as are the American infant songs. However, the common pattern of the Hungarian songs is *so* to *la,* a major second, followed by a minor third, *so-mi.*

Example:

American children's songs consistently contain the rising perfect fourth on an unstressed beat.

Example:

The choice of beginning notes in each case is *so-mi-la*. Only the order of interval teaching need be different. In American schools the *mi* to *la* interval should be taught with the *so* to *la* interval, because of the frequency with which the former occurs in our song material and because it exists in the common singing vocabulary of young American children.

Hungarian early childhood songs are, like American early childhood songs, frequently pentatonic in character, with the *fa*, if it occurs at all, present only as a passing tone in a descending line at the end of the song. These children's songs in Hungary, as in America, are generally *do*-centered or major in mode. On the other hand, the folk songs of Hungary, as separate from the infant and early childhood songs, are almost entirely *la*-centered or minor in mode, while minor-mode American folk songs are rare. Superficially this might seem to indicate a need for changing the sequence of the Method to suit the largely major-mode American folk song material. However, a closer look * at American folk materials shows that our pentatonic, pentachordal, and hexachordal music, although largely major in mode, contains the same basic scale ambit as the Hungarian minor modal folk music. That is, most of our folk music ranges from the low *so* and low *la* to the high *so* and high *la* rather than, as one might expect, from *do* to *do*. The principal difference between Hungarian and American folk music lies in the feeling of the mode and in the final notes: *la* in most Hungarian songs, *do* in most American ones. The ambit is the same for both. Since the Hungarian melodic sequence places *do* immediately after the *so-mi-la* pattern, and the low *la* and low *so* next, it is as well suited to American folk song as to Hungarian.

Rhythmically, one pattern that must be taught early in Hungary, because of its frequency in the folk music, is the eighth followed by the dotted quarter (♪ ♩.). This pattern is so rare in American folk music that it can be taught much later. On the other hand, sixteenth notes (▤ , ▤ , and ▤), uncommon in Hungarian songs, are so frequent in American music that they must be taught fairly early.

The greatest area of difference in rhythm is to be found in $\frac{6}{8}$ meter,

---

* These findings are based on the author's analysis of more than 1,000 American children's songs and folk songs and of several hundred Hungarian ones.

common to great amounts of American folk material but almost un-known in Hungary. Quite obviously, $\frac{6}{8}$ must be introduced on the con-scious level to children in American schools as soon as they have the necessary competency to handle it, i.e., as soon as they thoroughly under-stand both duple and triple simple meters ($\frac{2}{4}$, $\frac{3}{4}$, $\frac{2}{8}$, $\frac{3}{8}$). On the subcon-scious or rote level, American children should experience $\frac{6}{8}$ meter as early as possible, in kindergarten or grade one, for instance. It is the rhythm of our language, as much as the pronounced duple is the rhythm of the Hungarian language.

In deciding where to make small shifts in the sequence of skill-teaching to suit differences in American materials, the author consulted with sev-eral Hungarian authorities. The consensus was that in the final analysis the sequence *must* come from the materials themselves. This was how the Method evolved in Hungary and this is how it must evolve in America. The differences in song literature between Hungary and America present no insoluble problems.

Successful implementation of the Kodály concept in America is cer-tainly somewhat dependent upon finding sufficient folk songs and good composed songs to fit into the sequence of concepts and skills which comprise the Method. Materials exist! There are great numbers of Ameri-can petatonic, pentachordal, hexachordal, and modal folk songs and children's songs, many of them already collected and published by such people as William Wells Newell, John and Alan Lomax, Ruth Crawford Seegar, Richard Chase, and Edith Fowke. As for composed music, there are many suitable songs by Mozart, Schubert, Beethoven, *et al*, available in published collections for children. The recently-released Julliard Repertory Library offers perhaps the most comprehensive collection, in-cluding art music of every period, selected specifically for school children.

It remains, however, to select, analyze, categorize, and arrange such folk and art material into a teaching sequence. American collections are often annotated with respect to the locale and known history of the song, but are not analyzed musically in terms of rhythm, meter, mode, scale, and ambit, as are the Hungarian collections. Thus, using them demands a high level of musical proficiency on the part of the American teacher, who must know which songs are appropriate for what musical teaching purpose.

It should be remembered also that the major song series written for school use are filled with folk music and art music of recognized com-posers and provide a further readily-available source of materials. Again, these are not organized or arranged for the teaching sequence of Kodály. In every instance the teacher must possess the skill and knowledge to select and organize the music into the concept sequence of the method. There is still another aspect of the materials problem to be considered. In Hungary the first folk songs used with young children, after the nursery-type songs, are those of his own village or town, then of the small geographical area around his town, then of Hungary, then of the countries around Hungary closely related through their history and common peoples, and last, of the outside world. This approach from immediate and familiar to more distant and less familiar has been used for many years in American schools in the teaching of social sciences. In Hungary this approach has great validity since the population is a comparatively stationary one. A child born in Györ will probably go to school in Györ, marry in Györ, and die in Györ. The folk songs of Györ are a reasonable place to begin his musical education. However, the child born in San Francisco or Philadelphia may well have lived in three states even before beginning school. While some areas of the United States, particularly the South and Midwest, have a reasonably stable population, it is still a rare elementary school class in which there are not some children recently moved from other cities, towns, and states. Mobility of population is a part of the American way of life. With such mobility in American school life it would seem unnecessary to emphasize "Baltimore" folk songs for children in Baltimore schools and "St. Louis" folk songs for children in St. Louis schools. Yet there are authorities qualified in the Kodály Method who insist that such must be the case simply because it is so in Hungary.

Such insistence seems to indicate a lack of understanding of the complexities of the American social scene. Agreed, folk music is a good vehicle for teaching the skills of music literacy to young children; moreover, the folk music first taught should be that of the mother tongue. Other than this language requirement there seems little reason to restrict American schools to regional music at the beginning simply because such is the practice in Hungary. Many American folk songs may actually be traced back to earlier French, German, English, and other European versions, which came to this country with immigrants from those countries. In view of our multicultural and mobile society, the geographical approach to song materials simply does not seem valid for American schools. If one discards the geographical approach and uses good folk songs which suit the pedagogical purpose, then the problem of locating materials becomes much simpler.

To summarize: There are three basic problems to be solved in relation to materials of the Method in American schools:

1. The differences between American and Hungarian folk songs and how these differences affect the sequencing of skills,

2. The difficulties of finding, selecting, analyzing, and categorizing American folk material according to teaching purposes,

3. The decision as to whether to observe or to discard as inappropriate to American schools the Hungarian teaching sequence of songs from geographically near to more distant.

The third point can only be a matter of personal conviction, but the first and second need some years and much more research to be authoritatively answered.

Conclusions

No approach to teaching is without its related problems. The problems inherent in the Kodály Method in America are not insoluble, but coping with them will require time and thought on the part of every teacher who wishes to use the Method effectively. The Kodály Method is achieving some remarkable results in terms of pupil interests and abilities in various parts of the United States, but in each case the teachers involved are thorough musicians and fine teachers dedicated to making the system work.

The Kodály Method cannot be everyone's answer. For the teacher who is uncomfortable with *sol-fa* syllables and is unwilling to learn, for the teacher who feels that the strict structure of the Method is a straitjacket, for the teacher who believes that music reading should be taught through instruments rather than through voice, the Kodály Method will not be a reasonable choice. In our school music systems, where what to teach and how to teach it are largely left to the individual music teacher, it is the teacher who must make the final decision as to the appropriateness of the Method to his school system, his school, his children, and to himself. The Kodály Method is spreading in America. But it is spreading from interested teacher to interested teacher. If it is a revolution in the teaching of music, then it is one at the grass-roots level, where teachers and children are immediately involved.

Most good teachers of music have the same basic goals for their children. They wish to produce children who love music and who can work with music knowledgeably and comfortably. They hope to make music a known language to children. In achieving this goal, the Kodály Method has proved itself effective, not just in America but over much of the rest of the world. No other way of teaching music has had such impact on world music education in the twentieth century.

part 3

Lesson Planning

chapter 11

Lesson Planning

The lack of materials selected and organized into the framework of the Method has long been a stumbling block to the development of the Kodály Concept in the United States. To find the best songs for each new note, each new rhythm pattern; to find songs which in each case contain no unknown elements except the one new note or rhythm, is a time-consuming business. It is for this reason that the following songs are included in this volume. They represent a number of years of research, collection, and testing with children. Each of these songs has been used successfully with children for the teaching purpose suggested.

The songs are not meant to be a total music curriculum. Certainly, in the course of five or six elementary school years, many other songs would be taught. These songs have been the core of the curriculum followed by the author. They are arranged in the sequence of the Method and offer a guide to both the kinds of musical materials required and the manner of choosing and sequencing materials. Authentic infant songs, singing games, and folk music comprise the largest part of the collection. Some composed music has been used in the later section.

One of the most important aspects of the Kodály Method as practiced in Hungary is the extensive planning required of teachers. Each teacher must plan in advance a year's work for each grade. There is a general overall plan showing what skills and concepts are to be covered in a given grade, and another highly specific plan of lesson-by-lesson skills and concepts, including the materials and techniques to be used. These specific plans may be kept in detail only a few weeks ahead of the class progress, but the overall plan must be constantly referred to so that no skill is neglected or accidently overlooked.

Both the yearly plan and the detailed lesson-by-lesson program are kept in chart form in notebooks. Each teacher has her own format, but, in general, the headings are, as might be expected, quite similar. Márta Nemesszeghy, at the Zoltán Kodály School in Kecskemét used the following breakdown in listing the areas to be included in a year's work:

Melodic Elements	Artistic Performance
Rhythm Elements	Form
Tempi	Creative Ability
Dynamics	Song Material Types
Scales	Music Listening and History
Intervals and Chords	Text (words)
Part Singing	Books Used

Using the above list as headings, she lists the work of grade three, for example, as follows:

Melodic Elements: fi, ta, si; the natural; two sharps; two flats.

Rhythm Elements:

heterometric rhythms: $\frac{4}{4} + \frac{2}{4}$, $\frac{3}{4} + \frac{2}{4}$, $\frac{3}{4} + \frac{4}{4}$.

Tempi: moderato; andante; allegro.

Dynamics: f; ff.

Scales: do and *la* endings; *re* and *so* modes.

Intervals and Chords: major and minor thirds; major and minor seconds; perfect fifth; ascending and descending.

Part Singing: canons; Kodály's "Bicinia"; ostinati (rhythmic and melodic); line interweaving between alto and soprano.

Artistic Performance: clear singing; singing for understanding of words; relation of melody to text; feeling of mood in songs.

Form: Analyze the construction of familiar songs and fifth-jumping tunes; write as well as analyze four-phrase melodies; determine whether phrases are like or unlike, or similar but not identical; individually determine song forms such as A–B–B variant–A.

Creative Ability: Given the scale and the form, compose four-phrase songs (*re* ending, *la* ending, *do* ending, etc.).

Song Material Types: folk songs and composed songs; some two-voiced songs.

Music Listening and History: Differentiate between soprano and alto, high and low voices; identify instruments and chorus types; identify instrument families by name.

Text (words): Correlate with work in other subjects.

Books Used: Ének Zene 3; Kodály's *333 Sight-Singing Exercises, 100 Pentatonic Songs, Let us Sing Correctly,* "Bicinia" *(selected volume).*

Only the new material for the grade is listed in this outline. Thus, under dynamics, f and ff are shown, but the children would also review the mp, p, pp taught in earlier grades.

While it is self-evident that this kind of outline for the work of a grade is of itself helpful, it is not sufficient, since no sequence is given, no specific song materials mentioned, and no teaching procedures suggested. For these, the specifics of teaching, a more detailed type of planning is necessary. An efficient format is the following one, developed by Anna Hamvas at the Alsoerdosor Singing Primary School in Budapest. In tabular form Mrs. Hamvas lists, for each class:

Lesson Number	Inner Hearing
Procedure	Writing
Preparation for New Learning in Rhythm	Position of *do* (key)
Preparation for New Learning in Melody	Reading
Making Conscious New Skill in Rhythm	Ostinato
Making Conscious New Skill in Melody	Part Work

Not all headings have material listed under them for every lesson, but the existence of the headings makes clear to the teacher at a glance whether some important aspect of music learning has been neglected in a given number of lessons.

The column headed "Preparation" is a particularly important one. It is the feeling in Hungary that as a general rule six to eight songs are necessary for teaching one new concept or skill. Taking the note *re* as an example, the children would learn, by rote, four or five songs in which the only unknown note was *re*. Then, from one of these rote-taught songs the *re* would be derived with the class and "made conscious." After the lesson in which *re* was made a conscious learning to the children, all the previously learned *re* songs would be returned to and the place of *re* in each derived. Then in following lessons two or three new songs with *re* would be read, or taught by rote and their notation derived. This last step, although it does not occur on the lesson-plan tables, is consistently observed in Hungarian singing schools and has been referred to in this book as "concept or skill reinforcing."

In order to demonstrate the application of such planning to American school situations, three consecutive lessons for second grade are shown on page 133, using the Hungarian headings but with American materials inserted.

The column labelled "Procedure" stands ahead of all the others on such a planning chart, but it has been omitted here since it is difficult to put one's procedures in so small a space and still have them intelligible to others. As an alternative, a detailed lesson plan is given below, showing one order in which the materials, concepts, and skills listed for Lesson 10 might be given. In presentation there is certainly much room for individual difference among teachers. No one way is right. What follows is merely intended as a guide.

Grade 2. Lesson 10:

Purpose

This is a preliminary lesson on the note *re*. Its purpose is to prepare the children to hear and sing the note correctly in songs; in later lessons they will identify the note by its sound, its name, and its place in the scale of other known notes. All of the songs in the lesson prepare for the intervals of *re*. Even the rhythm work is tied into this purpose through the ostinato with "Hot Cross Buns."

Procedure

1. Review song: "Hot Cross Buns" (*m-r-d*).

   Sing, tapping beat;
   Sing, clapping rhythm;
   Sing, clápping ostinato | ⁀ | ⁀

2. Flash card rhythm exercise. Each flash card contains an eight-beat phrase from a familiar duple-meter song, in stem notation, using only ♩ , ♫ , ⁀. Children repeat the rhythms, clapping and saying rhythm duration syllables. Answers are given both by the whole class and by individual children. The last pattern,

   is from the song "Closet Key" and leads into:

3. *Game*—I have Lost My Closet Key (*m-r-d*). Children sing the song and play the game. There is individual singing on the last verse by children who "find the key" in the game. After finishing the game, the children sing the song slowly, using *sol-fa* and hand signs on the known sections and a hum for the unknown note.

4. Songs: "Ding Dong" (*m-d*). The children

   (a) Sing this rhythmic clapping game and do the game motions,
   (b) Sing the song with *sol-fa* syllables and hand signs,

Lesson Number	Prepare Rhythm	Prepare Melody	Make Conscious Rhythm	Make Conscious Melody	Reinforce Rhythm	Reinforce Melody	Inner Hearing	Writing	Position of *do*	Ostinato	Part Work
10		*re* songs: Closet Key; Hot Cross Buns; Sleep, Baby, Sleep; Hop, Old Squirrel			Patterns of ‖ ⊓ 𝄼 ‖ from familiar songs. Use flash cards.	*m-d* interval. Song: Ding Dong.	Sing: Ding Dong once aloud; then silently, ending together on words "Hot Dog" aloud.	Last phrase of Ding Dong. Ledger lines.	*C-do*	‖ 𝄼 𝄼 ‖ with Hot Cross Buns	
11	𝅗𝅥 Hot Cross Buns; Sleep, Baby, Sleep	*re* songs: as above plus Grandma Grunts		*re* Hot Cross Buns	Familiar patterns of ‖ ⊓ 𝄼 ‖ Listen, clap back, and say.			*re* Hot Cross Buns (whole song)	*F-do*	‖ 𝄼 𝄼 ‖ with Hop, Old Squirrel	
12			𝅗𝅥	Sleep, Baby, Sleep		*re* What'll We Do with the Baby? (*s-mrd*). New rote song. Review of all songs with *re*.		*re* Sleep, Baby, Sleep. First two phrases 𝅗𝅥 ⊓ *m r r d*	*G-do*	‖ ⊓ 𝄼 ‖ with Hop, Old Squirrel	Sleep, Baby, Sleep as a canon

(c) Derive the rhythm of the last phrase with the teacher,

(d) Place the last phrase of the song in staff notation in C-*do* at their desks (manuscript books or felt staves), being careful to place *do* on the ledger line below the staff,

(e) Sing the song again, looking and pointing to their written notes of the last phrase as they sing.

5. New song: "Sleep, Baby, Sleep" (*s-mrd*). Taught by rote by the teacher. The teacher sings the song with attention to artistry and phrasing.
The children

(a) Sing it back, one phrase at a time,

(b) Sing the entire song, with the teacher's voice helping where necessary.

Attention is given to the dynamics and to the lullaby quality of the song.

6. Review song with game: "Hop, Old Squirrel" (*m-r-d*).

This lesson takes about forty minutes with an average second-grade class. If less time is available, some of the material will have to be eliminated. However, it is very important that the children's games not be omitted. They are the joy of the music to young children. It would be better to drop one entire section from the lesson plan than to skip the games and try to cover all the skill material. In the lesson given either #4 or #5 could be postponed until the next lesson without damaging the continuity of the lesson or of the learning.

It sometimes happens that in trying to teach musical skills, teachers become so pressured that they forget the importance of musical enjoyment. The emphasis placed upon rote material in Hungary is due to the realization that if music does not give pleasure to children, the teaching of skills is pointless. There is in any good Hungarian music lesson a balance between singing, clapping, playing, thinking, and writing. It would be well to try to maintain such a balance here.

Because games are so much a part of early childhood music, the teacher should have some knowledge of basic singing game types; they are the same over most of the world. Basically they are of six types:

1. Circle games ("Here We Go Round the Mulberry Bush"),
2. Tag or chasing games ("Cat and Mouse"),
3. Counting-out games ("Eenie, Meenie, Miny-Moe"),
4. Partner games (involving choosing or social confrontation: "Patty-Cake, Patty-Cake"),
5. Bridge games ("London Bridge Is Falling Down"),
6. Games of hide and seek (involving children or objects: "The Closet Key").

Most singing games fit into one of these categories, although some are combinations. For example, "A Tisket, A Tasket" is both a circle game and a tag game. The games are rarely exact. Variations are found from one part of the country to another, and children enjoy inventing their own variants. Not all of the early childhood songs involve games, but wherever one is implied by the words, it should be played.

chapter 12

The Pedagogical Use of the Songs

The songs in this section have been notated in the way they would be shown to children—that is, nothing appears on the musical page that would not be within the musical knowledge of the child at the time he sees it. In the earliest songs only the number of beats in a measure is shown where the meter sign normally occurs. All the songs to be used in first and second grades are notated in C-, F-, and G-*do*. No key signatures are used, since no sharps or flats occur in pentatonic music in these keys.

The *sol-fa* scale of each song is given, in descending order, on the upper left hand corner of most songs. When a song is to be used only for teaching rhythmic concepts, the rhythm to be taught is shown rather than the scale. With these songs ("Skip to My Lou," for example) children should see only stem rhythm notation rather than staff notation, since the song contains *fa* and *ti,* notes unknown to the children at that point.

Musically, the first twelve songs contain only the notes *so, mi,* and *la,* and rhythm patterns using only quarter notes, pairs of eighth notes, and quarter rests. They may be taught by rote and used as game or action songs first. Later the tonal patterns of *so-mi* and *la* would be taught from them and the various rhythm patterns derived and constructed with rhythm duration sticks.

Song #1. This old wishing verse is most often sung on a chanting minor third by children, although occasionally they put in the fourth *m-l* at the words "star I" and "wish I." If this occurs it is best to allow the variation and simply consider the song as a three-note rather than a two-note one. The initial rhythm pattern, ♩ ♩ ♩ ♩, is a good one for establishing the feeling of the beat.

Song #2. In this counting-out song the usual words of the first verse are "buckle my shoe," but the word "tie" has been substituted to give two eighth notes rather than two sixteenth notes and an eighth. In all subsequent verses the eighth note pattern falls naturally. The children tap the beat to this song on their laps, using large motions as they sing. Later it may be used in a counting-out process to determine who will be "it" in a game.

Song #3. The cuckoo call gives a natural minor third. Children may sing this song in pairs, one singing the "cuckoo" part, the other singing "Where are you?" A game similar to Blind Man's Buff may be played with it. The only clue to the whereabouts of the prey is the repeated "cuckoo."

Song #4. This clapping game is useful both for the *s-m* interval and also for the rhythm pattern | | ♫ | common to many early childhood songs. The words given the motions.

Song #5. "Quaker, How Is Thee?" is a partner question and answer game. The teacher sings the question-phrases to a child; he responds with the answers. At the end of the fourth phrase he turns to another child and sings the question-phrases. This game can be played through several times, giving the teacher an opportunity to hear whether individual children are singing the minor third in tune.

Song #6. In "Hey, Hey, Look at Me" again there is opportunity for individual singing. The children insert any word they wish for "smiling" and perform a suitable action. Some additional verses could include dancing, frowning, hopping, skipping. This is played as a circle game, with the group stepping to the beat while the child who is "it" stands in the center. After he sings his verse, the whole group sings it, repeating his action.

Song #7. "Rain, Rain, Go Away" is one of the best known three-note songs in America. Children enjoy making new verses to add to the old two-line verse. The second verse given here was created by a first-grade youngster. The rhythm pattern | | ♫ | occurs at the beginning of the song and the *mi-la* fourth is on an unstressed beat, as it most frequently occurs in American children's songs.

Song #8. "The Mill Wheel" is useful for teaching the *so-la* second and the quarter rest. There are many delightful "miller" and "mill wheel" games and rhymes, most of which involve the miller grabbing a handful of the grain and then being chased by the person for whom he was grinding the meal. This simple version may be played as a circle game, with the miller in the center of the circle and the owner of the corn outside the circle ready to give chase at the end of the song.

Song #9. "Bye, Baby Bunting" should be sung quietly, its lullaby quality being emphasized. The *mi-la* interval in the first measure and the | ⊓ | | rhythm pattern will be used for teaching purposes after the song is learned.

Song #10. The "pocket" in this song refers to a pocketbook or purse. One child hides his eyes. A small purse is passed from child to child around the room while the class sings. On the word "it" at the end of the song the child holding the purse must hide it quickly, putting it in his pocket or desk, or even sitting on it. The child who was "it" has three guesses as to who has the purse.

Song #11. "The Clock" exists as a children's song in the U.S. and in Europe. It may be accompanied by one or two pairs of rhythm sticks playing a steady quarter-note beat in imitation of the ticking of a clock. The ⊓ ⸿ pattern is an unusual one and should be isolated and taught with rhythm duration syllables.

Song #12. A trotting or prancing step may be used to accompany "Bell Horses." Jingle clogs or jingle bells also add interest if only one or two pairs are used. More will make too much sound and cause children's singing to become harsh. The | ⊓ | ⊓ pattern of this song is uncommon and should be derived with children and constructed with sticks or written.

Song #13. "A Tisket, A Tasket" may be used only as a rote song because it begins with an upbeat. However, its three-note ambit and its traditional game of chase make it one that should be sung with children. The repeated singing while playing the game helps to reinforce the *so-mi-la* intervals. It may be used also for stepping to the beat. There are numerous versions of the game. All seem to involve a circle. One child walks around the circle and taps another on the shoulder. He gives chase and they race to see who can get back into the vacant place in the circle. In some versions the two children run in opposite directions. The loser becomes "it" for the next game.

The next three songs (#14, #15, #16) may be used to prepare children for learning *do*. In each case the final note of the song is *do* and the only other notes in the song are *so, mi,* and *la*. There are no rhythmic complications, so it would be possible, in addition, to use these songs for rhythm dictation.

Song #17. This Afro-American singing game may be used at this stage only as a rote song because of its rhythmic difficulties. However, the repeated major third is useful for practicing the *mi-do* interval. The game is a partner patty-cake type. Two children sway their heads from side to side on each "ding dong" and clap hands, first their own, then each other's, on the other words. At the end, on "Hot dog!", they clap their own hands sharply. The game starts slowly and increases in speed for three or four verses.

Song #18. This song is a good one through which to make *do* conscious to children. The words are traditional American ones, although the tune is Hungarian. Curiously enough, the Hungarian words also concern a cat and mouse chase game.

Songs #19, #20. The traditional children's song "Marching" presents the *do-mi-so* pattern in an ascending position, while "The Curfew Song" gives practice on the *do-so* fifth. Both these songs should be derived in staff notation with children.

Song #21. "Bells In the Steeple" can be sung only as a rote song at this point because it is in triple meter. However, the repeated ascending *do-mi-so* pattern will help to reinforce those intervals.

Song #22. In its simplest form "Tidy-O" is a circle game in which some children raise their joined hands to form windows while others weave in and out. Because the song contains no rhythmic complications and no intervals which have not previously been learned, it could be used as a total music reading experience.

The next four songs (#23 to #26) may be used to prepare the children for *re*.

Song #23. "The Closet Key" is accompanied by a game in which one youngster hides the key in the classroom and another must find it. The class offers musical clues by singing softly when he is far from the key and gradually singing louder as he gets closer to it. When he finds the key, he sings the last verse, "I have found," alone.

Song #24. This French Creole song may be used only for rote reinforcement of the *mi-re-do* pattern, since it is in triple meter.

Song #25. "Hop, Old Squirrel" is a nonsense song. Since it contains no melodic or rhythmic difficulties, children will be able later to place the entire song in staff notation.

Song #26. The song "Hot Cross Buns" is a good one for making *re* a conscious learning because of its descending line, repetition, and simple rhythms.

Song #27. The spiritual "Good News" can be a total reading song once the *re* has been learned. Children enjoy substituting other words for "chariot," depending upon the time of year. They may sing "Good news, winter's coming" or "summer's coming."

Song #28. "Grandma Grunts" is another easy reading song, although the humor of the words might be better served by treating it as a rote song initially, and deriving the *sol-fa* later.

The next nine songs (#29 to #37) contain only the now familiar four notes *so, mi, re,* and *do*. Some of these songs may be used for total reading, and others taught by a rote or rote-note process. Only three of them —"Hello Girls," "The Fountain," and "Old Blue"—contain any rhythmic complications. From these three songs, only the phrases with previously taught rhythms should be used for reading and writing.

The basic pentaton, *do, re, mi, so, la,* is the scale of the next seven songs (#38 to #44). There is nothing new in them melodically. "Here Comes a Bluebird," "Button," and "What'll We Do with the Baby?" are all possible reading songs. The others should be taught by rote and may be returned to later and their notation derived after syncopation, dotted rhythms, and sixteenth notes have been taught. Two of these songs have associated games.

Song #38. "Here Comes a Bluebird" is a partner-choice circle game. The child who is "it" stands in the circle, chooses his partner, skips around the circle with her, and then joins the circle, leaving her in the center of the circle ready to choose a new partner.

Song #39. "Button" is an object hiding game and may be played in the same fashion as "The Closet Key."

Song #40. A waltz-type varsovienne step is traditional to "Coffee Grows on White Oak Trees." It may be done as a partner dance or as a set of four couples facing each other in square-dance formation.

Song #41. The question-answer song "Anybody Pass Here?" gives much opportunity for individual singing. The child singing the question may call the name of any of his classmates instead of "Liza." The child called response with "No, my friend" and "Don't tell me so!"

Song #42. "Goin' Down to Town" may be used as a reading song only after the eighth-sixteenth note combinations have been taught. The melodic line, however, is simple and may be derived aurally with the class.

Songs #43, #44. Both the Kentucky lullaby "What'll We Do with the Baby?" and the Texas song "Built My Lady a Fine Brick House" may be used as total reading songs.

Songs #45 to #49. The next new note to be taught is low *la.* The song "I Got a Letter" is a good one to use for this teaching since it has only *mi, re, do,* and low *la.* The sustained note on the low *la* preceding the *do* also helps to establish that tonal relationship in children's ears. The songs following it may all be used for teaching or for reinforcing low *la.* The only unknown melodic element in any of them is the low *mi* in the last phrase of "The Canoe Song." The sixteenth-eighth note combinations (in "Land of the Silver Birch") and syncopation should be taught soon after this. "I Got a Letter," "The Canoe Song," and "Anybody Pass Here?" all contain examples of syncopation.

Songs #50 to #55. To introduce low *so* several songs are needed with both the low *la* and the low *so* in order that the children may discover the place of low *so* below low *la.* Either the sea chantey "I've Been to Haarlem" or the spiritual "Now Let Me Fly" is a good choice for this purpose because of the initial *do, la,, so,* descending line. Possible preparatory songs are "Cotton-Eye Joe," "The Old Grey Goose," and "Here She Comes, So Fresh and Fair." The Southern lullaby "Hush, Little Baby" is useful to teach the *so,-re* and *so,-mi* intervals.

Songs #56, #57. Rhythmically the children should by now have had $\frac{2}{4}$ and $\frac{4}{4}$ meters and be ready for $\frac{3}{4}$. They should have had eighth notes, quarter notes, half notes, and whole notes, as well as syncopation. They are ready for sixteenth notes, which may be derived from already familiar songs such as "Skip to My Lou" and "Love Somebody." Since neither of these songs is pentatonic, only the rhythm should be shown to them for teaching purposes at this point. After the four sixteenth-note group and the sixteenth-eighth note combinations have been taught, songs learned by rote earlier, containing sixteenth notes, may be returned to and read with *sol-fa* and rhythm duration syllables. These include "Tidy-O" (#22), "Goin' Down to Town" (#42), and "Land of the Silver Birch" (#48).

Songs #58, #59, #60. For initial teaching of triple meter, three songs —"Billy Barlow," "Lavender's Blue," and "O, How Lovely Is the Evening"—are recommended since none of them contains the anacrusis so common to $\frac{3}{4}$ meter in American folk music. After the meter is taught, the upbeat may be introduced and the songs in triple meter, learned earlier by rote, may be returned to and read from notation. These include "Bells in the Steeple" (#19), "Fais Do Do" (#24), and "Coffee Grows on White Oak Trees" (#40).

Songs #61 to #93. With all the notes of the extended pentaton now in their cognitive musical vocabulary, it is important that children have much opportunity for practice with this vocabulary before going farther melodically. These thirty-three songs are all based on the extended pentaton. They are arranged in order of increasing ambit, from musically simpler songs to more complex. Many of these songs may be read by children or taught by a rote-note process. Some of the rhythmically complicated ones, "Wayfaring Stranger" and "Child of God," for example, are still best taught by rote.

Songs #94 to #101 are pentatonic, but contain the high *do* (#94–#98), the high *re* and high *mi* (#99–#101). These last two notes do not occur frequently in American pentatonic folk music. Perhaps the range of a ninth or a tenth is not a comfortable one for folk singers. It is certainly not a comfortable one for children, although most third- and fourth-grade youngsters can sing these songs if they are encouraged to sing softly, without pushing. Specifically, for the *so-do'* interval, both "I Had Me a Bird" and "The Gambling Suitor" are good. The octave *do-do'* occurs frequently in "Hop Up, My Ladies." The *la-do'*, minor third occurs in "When the Train Comes Along," "The Gambling Suitor," "Billy Came over the Main White Ocean," and "Rain Come Wet Me." Other intervals with high *do* are infrequent and may be dealt with as they occur.

Songs #102 to #126 all include the note *fa*. They are arranged in order of scale complexity, not of teaching sequence. Many of these songs should be taught by rote in earlier grades. For example, "Juba," "Old Aunt

Kate," "Hanging Out the Linen Clothes," "Whistle, Daughter, Whistle," "Stars Shinin'," "Jimmy Rose," "This Old Man," "Brother John," "Fiddle-de-de," and "Punchinello" are all songs which would appeal to second- and third-grade children. They may then be returned to in fourth grade and used for teaching and reinforcing the note *fa*. Some composed songs are included in this group: "Joyful, Joyful" (Beethoven), "Da Pacem Domine," "Cradle Hymn" (Bach). This is in keeping with the Hungarian practice of including art-song material beginning in the middle grades.

For teaching *fa* the following songs are particularly recommended:

For their ascending or descending stepwise passage: "Whistle, Daughter, Whistle," "Joyful, Joyful," "Da Pacem Domine," "Cradle Hymn," "Stars Shinin'," "Christmas Greetings," "It Rained a Mist," "I Saw Three Ships," "Water, Water, Wildflowers," "This Old Man," "Brother John," and "Punchinello."

The minor third interval *fa-re* occurs in a strong position in "Old Aunt Kate," "Sometimes I Feel Like a Mournin' Dove," "Oranges, Lemons," and "Turn, Cinnamon, Turn."

Fa to *la,* the major third, may be practiced through "Fire Down Below" and "Jimmy Rose, He Went to Town." The latter is also good for practicing the less common *do* to *fa* perfect fourth.

Fa as a repeated tone occurs in "Joseph Dearest, Joseph Mild," "New River Train," "Fiddle-de-de," "The Old Chisholm Trail," and "Turn, Cinnamon, Turn."

There are many more songs given for *fa* than the usually recommended eight for each new interval. The half step *fa-mi* is a difficult one for children to sing in tune and much practice is needed with it.

The next eight songs (#127 to #134) have been chosen for teaching *ti* because they have limited scales and present the *ti* in both stepwise and skipwise passages. Only one of them, "Marching Down the Levee," is an American folk song. The others are foreign folk material or are composed songs. While there is no paucity of American folk material containing *ti,* it is most commonly used as a passing tone near the end of the song. This lack of importance within the song makes *ti* difficult to isolate and use for teaching purposes. In all but one of these eight songs the *ti* occurs several times, making it easier to isolate and teach. The *do-ti-la* ascending and descending scale patterns may be taught through the Praetorius round "Rise Up, O Flame," "The Birch Tree," "Hey, Ho, Nobody Home," and "Nightime." The *ti-re* minor third and the *ti-so* major third occur in "Marching Down the Levee" and the *ti-so* in the "Laughing Song." The *re-ti-so* occurs repeatedly as a broken triad in "I's the B'y." The Latin canon "Pauper Sum Ego" is included in this group of songs because it contains the *do-ti-do* half step twice.

Songs #135 to #148. Children now have all of the notes for singing songs written in the diatonic major scale (Ionian mode) and the pure minor scale (Aeolian mode). These fourteen songs have been selected to give practice in singing, reading, and writing within these modes. Most of them contain obvious stepwise scale passages. The children should, when note-reading, first derive the scale of the song on the board with the teacher. One song, "St. Anthony's Chorale" (Haydn), is given without words. Singing motifs by famous composers in *sol-fa* is practiced frequently in the upper grades of Hungarian schools. The themes of any composition to which the children are going to listen are sung in *sol-fa* before the composition is heard. In using this chorale a teacher might have the children first sing it, then hear either the Haydn choral setting or the Brahms variations on that setting. Songs #135 to #142 are major in mode, #143 to #148 are minor. They are arranged in this manner for ease of scale analysis by the teacher, and should be taught intermixed. When children are reading and writing fluently with the Ionian major and Aeolian minor scales, other modal scales and altered scales may be introduced through songs.

Songs #149 to #158. The last ten songs offered here contain examples of common scale alterations. One frequently-used mode in folk music is Mixolydian, basically a major scale with a flatted seventh (*ta*). The American folk songs "Old Joe Clark," "Poor Old Crow," and "The Jam on Gerry's Rocks" are all Mixolydian. "Sweet Water Rolling" is not as clear-cut an example since the seventh is unaltered in the third measure; however, its final phrase is certainly characteristically Mixolydian. "Haul Away, Joe" and "As I Roved Out" are both Dorian. They are essentially minor scales with a raised sixth (*fi*). "Ah, Poor Bird," "Go Down, Moses," and "Mam'zelle Zizi" are not modal but minor with a raised seventh (*si*). The three alterations presented in these songs—*ti* to *ta, fa* to *fi*, and *so* to *si*—are the only ones found frequently enough in song material to warrant much attention. The last song given, "By the Waters Babylon," an anonymous Tudor canon, contains both *ta* and *si*, but as decorative notes rather than as part of the basic scale.

It is hoped that these examples will serve as a guide to teachers searching for materials with which to use the Kodály Method. Certainly there are other suitable songs at every step. As better materials are found they should be added, or substituted for those given here. One of the principal purposes of this collection, after all, is to indicate the factors which must be examined in song selection.

The Songs

The Songs

1. THE WISHING SONG

s—m

Star - light star bright, First star I see to - night,

Wish I may, Wish I might, Have the wish I wish to - night.

2. THE COUNTING SONG

s—m

One, two, tie my shoe; Three, four, shut the door;
Five, six, pick up sticks; Seven, eight, lay them straight;
Nine, ten, big fat hen; 'Leven, twelve, dig and delve.

3. CUCKOO

s—m

Cuck - oo, where are you? Cuck - oo, where are you?

4. CLAP YOUR HANDS

s—m

Clap, clap, clap your hands, Clap your hands to - geth - er.
Stamp, Stamp, stamp your feet, Stamp your feet to - geth - er.

5. QUAKER, QUAKER

s—m

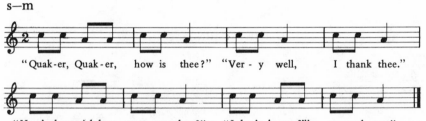

"Quak-er, Quak-er, how is thee?" "Ver - y well, I thank thee."

"How's thy neigh-bor next to thee?" "I don't know, I'll go and see."

From *Games and Songs of American Children* by William Wells Newell.
Dover Publications, Inc., New York, 1963.

6. LOOK AT ME

s—m

Hey! Hey! Look at me I am smil - ing, you can see!

7. RAIN, RAIN

l—s—m

Rain, Rain, go a - way; Come a - gain some oth - er day;
Sun - shine's here to stay, Now we can go out to play.

8. THE MILL WHEEL

l—s—m

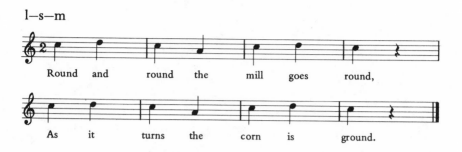

Round and round the mill goes round,

As it turns the corn is ground.

9. BYE BABY BUNTING

l—s—m

Bye ba - by bunt - ing Dad - dy's gone a - hunt - ing (to)

Catch a lit - tle rab - bit skin to wrap the ba - by bunt - ing in.

10. LUCY LOCKET

l—s—m

Lucy- y Lock - et lost her pock - et, Kit - ty Fish - er found it,
Not a pen - ny was there in it, on - ly rib - bon round it.

11. THE CLOCK

l—s—m

Tick - tock, tick - tock, goes the lit - tle clock,

Night and day it just goes tick - tock;

O - pen wide the door of the lit - tle clock,

"Cuck - oo," "Cuck - oo," "Cuck - oo," "Cuck - oo."

12. BELL HORSES

l—s—m

Bell hors - es, bell hors - es, What's the time of day?

One o - clock, two o - clock, Time to a - way!

13. A TISKET, A TASKET

l—s—m

A tisk - et a task - et, a green and yel - low bask - et,

I sent a let - ter to my love and on the way I lost it,

I lost it, I lost it, yes, on the way I lost it.

14. RING AROUND THE ROSY

l—s—m (d)

Ring a - round the ros - y, Pock-et full of pos - y,

Ash - es, ash - es, All fall down!

15. RISE, SALLY, RISE

l—s—m (d)

Here sits a mous - y, In her lit - tle housie,____

No one comes to see her ex - cept her grand-ma mousie,____

Rise, sal - ly, rise! Wipe out your eyes!

Turn to the east and turn to the west and

Turn to the one that you like best!

16. DING DONG DELL

l—s—m (d)

Ding - dong, ding - dong, ding - dong dell!

Who put pus - sy in the well?

Who put her in? Lit - tle John - ny green!

Who pulled her out? Lit - tle Tom - my stout!

17. I'VE GOT THE RHYTHM IN MY HEAD

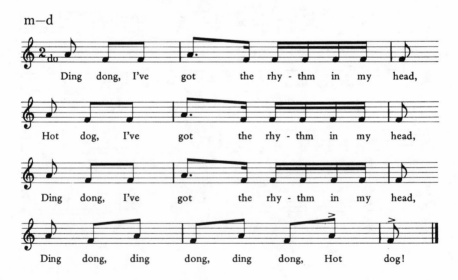

m—d

Ding dong, I've got the rhy - thm in my head,

Hot dog, I've got the rhy - thm in my head,

Ding dong, I've got the rhy - thm in my head,

Ding dong, ding dong, ding dong, Hot dog!

18. MOUSE MOUSIE

19. MARCHING

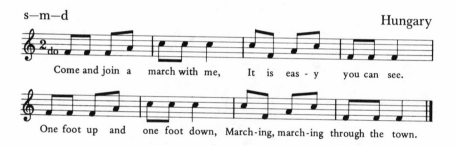

20. CURFEW SONG

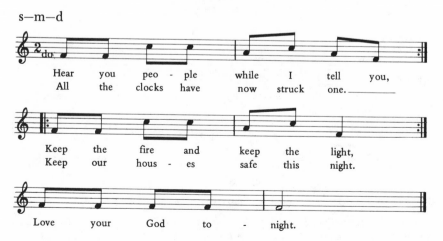

21. BELLS IN THE STEEPLE

s—m—d

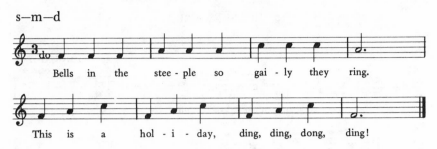

22. TIDY-O

l—s—m—d

23. CLOSET KEY

m—r—d

2. Help me find the closet key in my lady's garden.

3. I have found the closet key in my lady's garden.

From *American Folk Songs for Children* by Ruth Crawford Seeger. Reprinted by permission of Curtis Brown, Ltd. Copyright, 1948, by Ruth Crawford Seeger.

24. FAIS DO-DO

Fais do - do, and let us go dream - ing,

Fais do - do, come dream - ing with me.

25. HOP, OLD SQUIRREL

Hop, old squirrel, ei - dle - dum, ei - dle - dum,

Hop, old squirrel, ei - dle - dum, dee!

Hop, old squirrel, ei - dle - dum, ei - dle - dum,

Hop, old squirrel, ei - dle - dum, - dee!

From *American Folk Songs for Children* by Ruth Crawford Seeger. Reprinted by permission of Curtis Brown, Ltd. Copyright, 1948, by Ruth Crawford Seeger.

26. HOT CROSS BUNS

Hot cross buns! Hot cross buns!

One a pen - ny, two a pen - ny, Hot cross buns!

27. GOOD NEWS

m—r—d

Good news!   Char-iot's com-ing!   Good news!   Char-iot's com-ing!

Good news!   Char-iot's com-ing!   Don't leave me be - hind.

28. GRANDMA GRUNTS

m—r—d

Grand - ma   Grunts   said   a   cu - rious   thing,

"Boys   can   whis - tle   but   girls   must   sing,"

That   is   what   I   heard   her   say,

'Twas   no   lon - ger   than   yes - ter - day!

Boys   can   whis - tle,   *(whistling . . . .)*

Girls   must   sing,   Tra,   la,   la,   la,   la!

29. SLEEP, BABY, SLEEP

s mrd

Sleep, ba - by, sleep; Fa - ther tends the sheep;

Moth - er shakes the dream-land tree And down come all the

dreams for thee. Sleep, ba - by sleep.

30. OLD BLUE

s mrd

I had a dog and his name was Blue,_____

I had a dog and his name was Blue._____

I had a dog and his name was Blue,_____

And I bet - cha five dol - lars he's a good dog too.

Here_____ Blue! You good dog you.

2. Chased that possum up a hollow tree,
   Best huntin' dog you ever did see.

3. Caught that possum up a hollow tree,
   Best huntin' dog you ever did see.

4. Baked that possum good and brown,
   Laid sweet potaters all around.

5. Old Blue died, he died one day,
   So I dug his grave and I buried him away.

6. I dug his grave with a silver spade,
   Lowered him down with a golden chain.

7. When I get to heaven there's one thing I'll do,
   I'll grab me a horn and blow for Blue!

31. MARY HAD A LITTLE LAMB

s mrd

Mar - y had a   lit - tle lamb,   lit - tle lamb,   lit - tle lamb,

Mar - y   had a   lit - tle lamb whose   fleece was white as   snow.

32. THE FOUNTAIN

s mrd   French Canadian

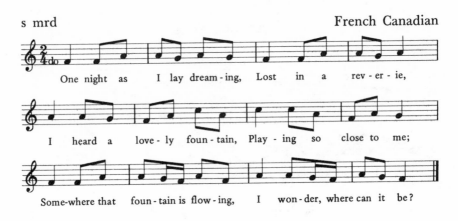

One night as   I lay dream - ing, Lost   in   a   rev - er - ie,

I   heard a   love - ly   foun - tain, Play - ing   so   close to   me;

Some-where that   foun - tain is flow - ing,   I   won - der, where can it   be?

33. JIM-ALONG JOSIE

s mrd   Traditional

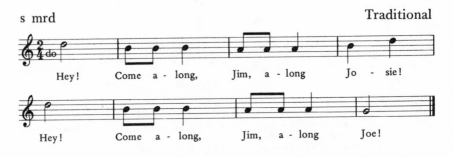

Hey!   Come a - long,   Jim, a - long   Jo - sie!

Hey!   Come   a - long,   Jim, a - long   Joe!

34. DANCE THE CAPUCINE

s mrd   French Canadian

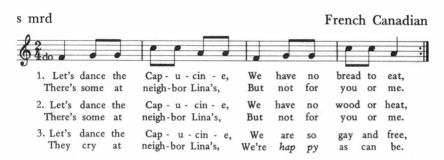

1. Let's dance the	Cap - u - cin - e,	We	have	no	bread	to	eat,
There's some at	neigh-bor Lina's,	But	not	for	you	or	me.
2. Let's dance the	Cap - u - cin - e,	We	have	no	wood	or	heat,
There's some at	neigh-bor Lina's,	But	not	for	you	or	me.
3. Let's dance the	Cap - u - cin - e,	We	are	so	gay	and	free,
They cry at	neigh-bor Lina's,	We're	*hap*	*py*	as	can	be.

35. HELLO, GIRLS!

s mrd   American Folk Song

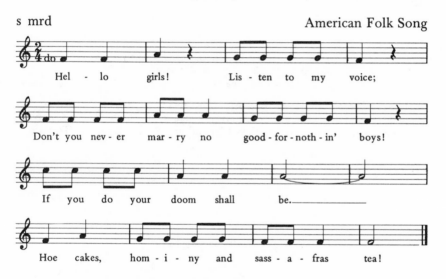

Hel - lo   girls!   Lis - ten to my voice;

Don't you nev - er   mar - ry no   good - for - noth - in'   boys!

If you do your doom shall be._____

Hoe cakes, hom - i - ny and sass - a - fras tea!

2. When a young man falls in love,
   First, it's "honey" and then "turtledove."
   After he's married, no such thing;
   "Get up and get my breakfast,
   You good-for-nothing thing!"

36. SWEETEST LITTLE BABY

s mrd

2. Mammy, mammy told me O.
   You're the meanest little rascal in the country O.
   I looked in the glass and found it so,
   Just as Mammy told me O.

From *Sally Go Round the Sun* by Edith Fowke. Copyright © 1969 by Mc-
Clelland & Stewart, Ltd. Reprinted by permission of Doubleday & Company,
Inc. and the Canadian publishers, McClelland and Stewart Limited, Toronto.

37. WHO'S THAT!

s mrd   Virginia

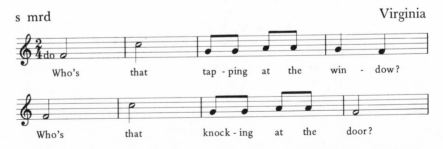

From *American Folk Songs for Children* by Ruth Crawford Seeger. Reprinted
by permission of Curtis Brown, Ltd. Copyright, 1948, by Ruth Crawford Seeger.

Mam - my tap - ping at the win - dow?

Pap - py knock - ing at the door.

38. HERE COMES A BLUEBIRD

ls mrd   Traditional

Here comes a blue - bird, In - to my gar - den,

Hi _____ Did - dle - um - a Day - Day - Day. _____

2. Takes a pretty partner into the garden,
   Hi_____ Diddle-um-a Day-Day-Day.

39. BUTTON

ls mrd   Traditional

But - ton, you must wan - der, wan - der, wan - der,

But - ton, you must wan - der ever - y - where,

Bright eyes will find you, sharp eyes will find you,

But - ton, you must wan - der ever - y - where.

40. COFFEE GROWS ON WHITE OAK TREES

ls mrd   Southern

Cof - fee   grows   on   white   oak   trees,

The   riv - er   flows   with   hon - ey   O,

Go   choose   some - one   to   roam   with   you,

As   sweet   as   'las   -   ses   can - dy   O.

41. ANYBODY' PASS HERE

ls mrd

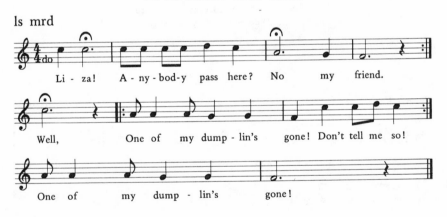

Li - za!   A - ny - bod-y   pass here?   No   my   friend.

Well,   One of   my dump - lin's   gone!   Don't tell me   so!

One   of   my   dump - lin's   gone!

42. GOIN' DOWN TO TOWN

ls mrd   Kentucky

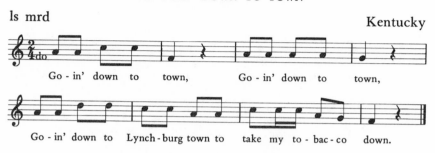

Go - in' down to   town,   Go - in' down to   town,

Go - in' down to Lynch - burg town to   take my to - bac - co   down.

2. Times a gettin' hard, money gettin' scarce,
   Pay me for them tobacco, boys, and I will leave this place.

3. Had an old grey horse, took him down to town,
   Sold him for a half a dollar, and only a quarter down.

From *American Folk Songs for Children* by Ruth Crawford Seeger. Reprinted by permission of Curtis Brown, Ltd. Copyright, 1948, by Ruth Crawford Seeger.

43. WHAT'LL WE DO WITH THE BABY?

ls mrd   Kentucky

What - 'll   we   do   with   the   ba - by?

What - 'll   we   do   with   the   ba - by?

What - 'll   we   do   with   the   ba - by?   Oh,   we'll

Wrap   it   up   in   ca - li - co,   Wrap   it   up   in

ca - li - co, and   send   it   to   its   pap - py - o!

From *American Folk Songs for Children* by Ruth Crawford Seeger. Reprinted by permission of Curtis Brown, Ltd. Copyright, 1948, by Ruth Crawford Seeger.

44. BUILT MY LADY A FINE BRICK HOUSE

ls mrd   Texas

From *American Folk Songs for Children* by Ruth Crawford Seeger. Reprinted by permission of Curtis Brown, Ltd. Copyright, 1948, by Ruth Crawford Seeger.

45. I GOT A LETTER

mrd l₁   South Carolina

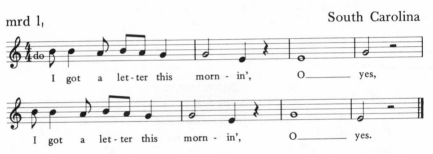

From *American Folk Songs for Children* by Ruth Crawford Seeger. Reprinted by permission of Curtis Brown, Ltd. Copyright, 1948, by Ruth Crawford Seeger.

46. OLD MISTER RABBIT

mrd l₁   Mississippi

47. CANOE SONG

mrd l, m,   Traditional

My pad - dles keen and bright, Flash-ing like sil - ver,

Fol - low the wild goose flight, Dip, dip and swing.___

2. Dip, dip and swing her back,
   Flashing like silver,
   Swift as the wild goose flies,
   Dip, dip and swing.

48. CRAWDAD HOLE

ls mrd l,   Carolina

You get a line and I'll bring a pole, hon - ey,_____

You get a line and I'll bring a pole, Ba - by._____

You get a line and I'll bring a pole,

We'll go fish - in' in a craw - dad hole,

Hon - ey___ ba - by o' mine._____

49. LAND OF THE SILVER BIRCH

ls mrd l,   Canadian

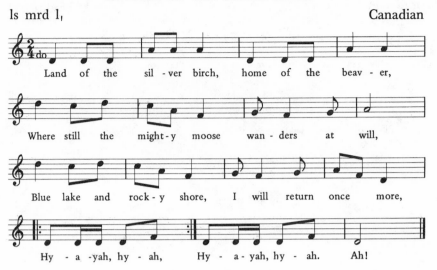

Land of the sil - ver birch, home of the beav - er,

Where still the might-y moose wan - ders at will,

Blue lake and rock - y shore, I will return once more,

Hy - a -yah, hy - ah, Hy - a - yah, hy - ah. Ah!

50. COTTON EYE JOE

mrd l, s,   Alabama

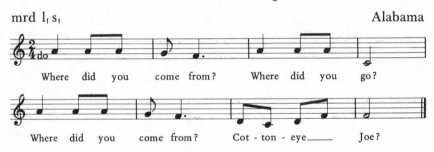

Where did you come from? Where did you go?

Where did you come from? Cot - ton - eye___ Joe?

2. Come for to see you,
   Come for to sing.
   Come for to show you
   My diamond ring.

51. OLD GRAY GOOSE

ls mrd l, s,

Southern Folk Song

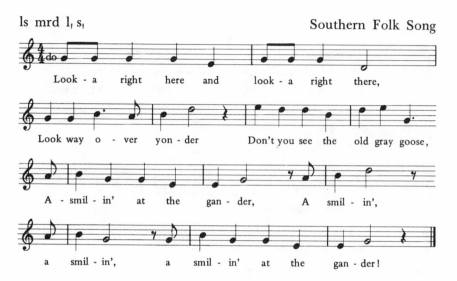

Look - a right here and look - a right there,

Look way o - ver yon - der Don't you see the old gray goose,

A - smil - in' at the gan - der, A smil - in',

a smil - in', a smil - in' at the gan - der!

52. HERE SHE COMES SO FRESH AND FAIR

s mrd l, s,

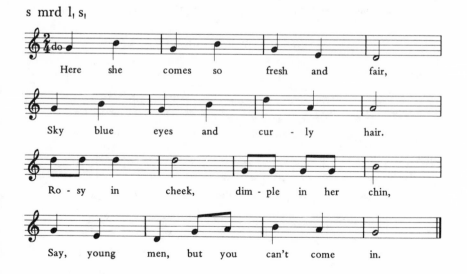

Here she comes so fresh and fair,

Sky blue eyes and cur - ly hair.

Ro - sy in cheek, dim - ple in her chin,

Say, young men, but you can't come in.

53. I'VE BEEN TO HAARLEM

ls mrd l₁s₁　　　　　　　　　　　　　　　　　　Sea Chantey

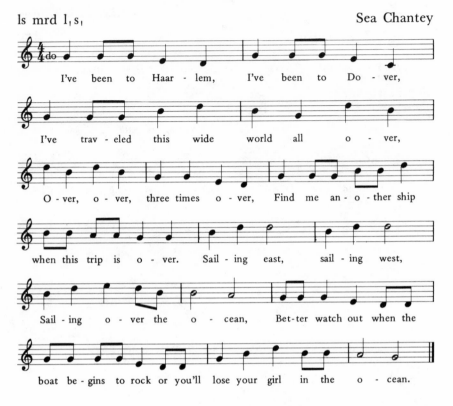

I've been to Haar - lem, I've been to Do - ver,

I've trav - eled this wide world all o - ver,

O - ver, o - ver, three times o - ver, Find me an - o - ther ship

when this trip is o - ver. Sail - ing east, sail - ing west,

Sail - ing o - ver the o - cean, Bet-ter watch out when the

boat be - gins to rock or you'll lose your girl in the o - cean.

54. NOW LET ME FLY

ls mrd l₁s₁　　　　　　　　　　　　　　　　　　Spiritual

Way down yon - der in the mid - dle of the field,

See me work - ing at the char - iot wheel.

Not so par - tic - 'lar 'bout work - ing at the wheel, But I

just went to see how the char - iot feels. Now

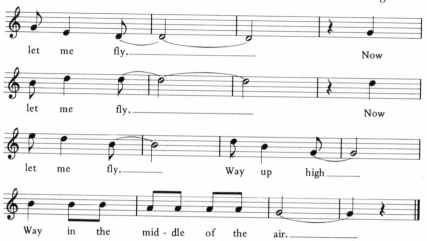

let me fly.⎯⎯⎯⎯⎯⎯⎯⎯⎯⎯⎯ Now

let me fly.⎯⎯⎯⎯⎯⎯⎯⎯⎯⎯⎯ Now

let me fly.⎯⎯⎯ Way up high⎯⎯

Way in the mid - dle of the air.⎯⎯⎯⎯

55. HUSH LITTLE BABY

mrd s₁   Southern

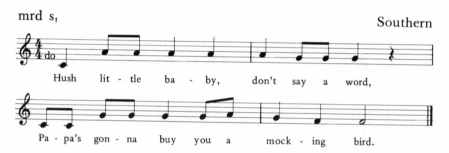

Hush lit - tle ba - by, don't say a word,

Pa - pa's gon - na buy you a mock - ing bird.

2. If that mocking bird won't sing,
   Papa's gonna buy you a diamond ring.

3. If that diamond ring turns brass,
   Papa's gonna buy you a lookin' glass.

4. If that lookin' glass gets broke,
   Papa's gonna buy you a billy goat.

56. LOVE SOMEBODY

Love some-bod-y, yes I do Love some-bod-y, yes I do

Love some - bod-y, yes I do Love some-bod-y, but I won't say who.

57. SKIP TO MY LOU

Fly's in the but-ter-milk, Shoo fly shoo, Fly's in the but-ter-milk,

Shoo fly shoo, Fly's in the but-ter-milk, Shoo fly shoo,

Skip to my Lou my dar - ling, Lou, Lou,

Skip to my Lou, Lou, Lou, Skip to my Lou,

Lou, Lou, Skip to my Lou, Skip to my Lou my dar - ling.

58. BILLY BARLOW

Texas

"Let's go hunt - ing," says Risk - y Rob,

"Let's go hunt - ing," says Ro - bin to Bob,

"Let's go hunt - ing," says Da - n'l to Joe,

"Let's___ go hunt - ing," says Bil - ly Bar - low.

59. LAVENDER'S BLUE

England

La - ven - der's blue, dil - ly, dil - ly, La - ven - der's green,

When you are king, dil - ly, dil - ly, I shall be Queen.

60. O, HOW LOVELY

Canon-England

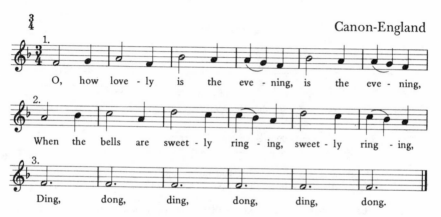

O, how love - ly is the eve - ning, is the eve - ning,

When the bells are sweet - ly ring - ing, sweet - ly ring - ing,

Ding, dong, ding, dong, ding, dong.

61. DOWN CAME A LADY

Virginia

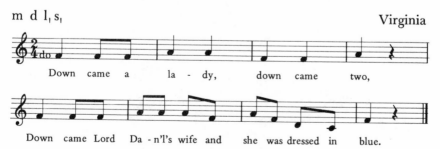

Down came a la - dy, down came two,

Down came Lord Da - n'l's wife and she was dressed in blue.

From *American Folk Songs for Children* by Ruth Crawford Seeger. Reprinted by permission of Curtis Brown, Ltd. Copyright, 1948, by Ruth Crawford Seeger.

62. PERRY MERRY DICTUM DOMINEE

mrd s₁   Appalachian

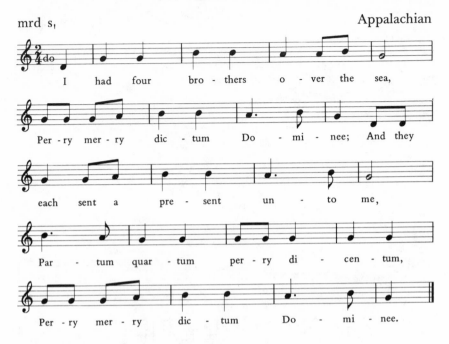

I had four bro - thers o - ver the sea,

Per - ry mer - ry dic - tum Do - mi - nee; And they

each sent a pre - sent un - to me,

Par - tum quar - tum per - ry di - cen - tum,

Per - ry mer - ry dic - tum Do - mi - nee.

2. The first sent me cherries without any stones. Perry. . . . .
   The second sent a chicken without any bones. Partum Quartum. . . . .

3. The third sent a blanket that had no thread. Perry. . . . .
   The fourth sent a book that could not be read. Partum Quartum. . . . .

4. When the cherries are in bloom they have no stones. Perry. . . . .
   When the chicken's in the egg it has no bone. Partum Quartum. . . . .

5. When the blanket's in the fleece, it has no thread. Perry. . . . .
   When the book's in the press, it cannot be read. Partum Quartum. . . . .

63. CHATTER WITH THE ANGELS

mrd l₁ s₁   Spiritual

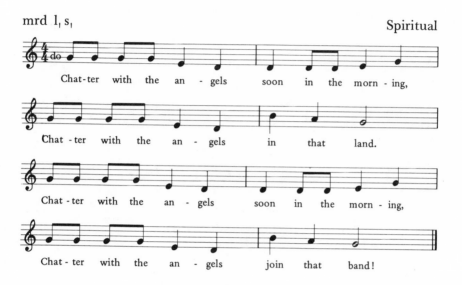

Chat-ter with the an - gels soon in the morn - ing,
Chat - ter with the an - gels in that land.
Chat - ter with the an - gels soon in the morn - ing,
Chat - ter with the an - gels join that band!

64. DUCKS IN THE MILLPOND

s mrd l₁ s₁   Virginia

Ducks in the mill - pond, a geese in the clo - ver, a
Fell in the mill - pond, a wet all o - ver.
Lawd, lawd____ gon - na get on a rink - tum,
Lawd, lawd____ gon - na get on a rink - tum.

From *American Folk Songs for Children* by Ruth Crawford Seeger. Reprinted by permission of Curtis Brown, Ltd. Copyright, 1948, by Ruth Crawford Seeger.

65. I GAVE MY LOVE A CHERRY

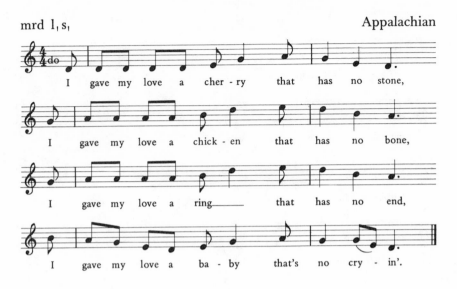

mrd l₁s₁   Appalachian

I gave my love a cher-ry that has no stone,

I gave my love a chick-en that has no bone,

I gave my love a ring____ that has no end,

I gave my love a ba-by that's no cry-in'.

2. How can there be a cherry that has no stone ! . . . (etc.)

3. A cherry when it's bloomin' it has no stone,
A chicken when it's peepin' it has no bone,
A ring when it's a-rollin' it has no end,
A baby when it's sleepin' is no cryin'.

66. THE SQUIRREL

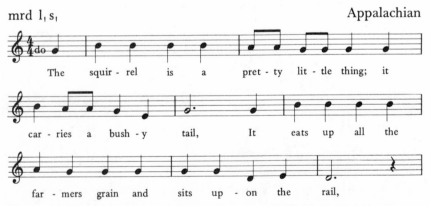

mrd l₁s₁   Appalachian

The squir-rel is a pret-ty lit-tle thing; it

car-ries a bush-y tail, It eats up all the

far-mers grain and sits up-on the rail,

From *English Folk Songs from the Southern Appalachians* (Cecil Sharp) by permission of Oxford University Press.

Ho! ho!_____ ho! ho! and sits up - on the rail.

2. The partridge is a pretty little bird;
   It carries a speckled breast.
   It steals away the farmer's grain,
   And carries it to its nest.
   Ho! Ho! Ho! Ho! And carries it to its nest.

3. The raccoon's tail is ringed around;
   The opossum's tail is bare.
   The rabbit's got no tail at all,
   But a little bunch of hair.
   Ho! Ho! Ho! Ho! But a little bunch of hair.

67. HEY, BETTY MARTIN

mrd l, s,

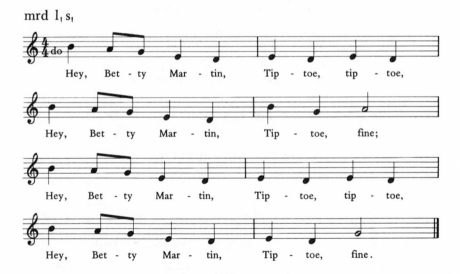

Hey, Bet - ty Mar - tin, Tip - toe, tip - toe,

Hey, Bet - ty Mar - tin, Tip - toe, fine;

Hey, Bet - ty Mar - tin, Tip - toe, tip - toe,

Hey, Bet - ty Mar - tin, Tip - toe, fine.

68. SWAPPING SONG

mrd l₁ s₁   Virginia

My fa-ther died but I don't know how,—
He left me a horse to hitch to the plow,—
To my wing-wong-wad-dle, To my jack-straw strad-dle!
And John-ny's got his fid-dle and he's gone on home!

2. I swapped my horse and got me a cow,
   And in that trade I just learned how.

3. I swapped my cow and got me a calf.
   And in that trade I lost just half.

4. I swapped my calf and got me a pig,
   The poor little thing it never growed big.

From *American Folk Tales and Songs* by Richard Chase. Dover Publications, Inc., New York, 1956. Reprinted through the permission of the publisher.

69. SCOTLAND'S BURNING

s mrd s₁   Traditional

Scot-land's burn-ing, Scot-land's burn-ing, Fetch the en-gines, Fetch the en-gines,
Fire! fire! fire! fire! Pour on wa-ter, Pour on wa-ter.

70. MY PAPPY, HE WILL SCOLD ME

s mrd s₁   Ozark Folk Song

My pap-py he will scold me, scold me, scold me,

My pap-py he will scold me for get - ting in a fight.

71. SWEEP AWAY

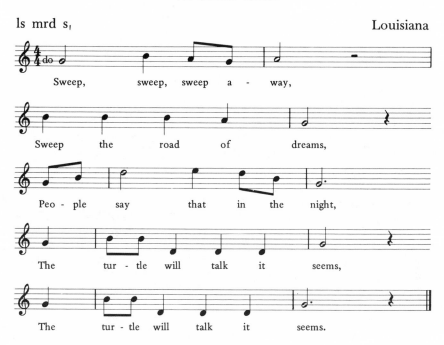

ls mrd s₁   Louisiana

Sweep, sweep, sweep a - way,

Sweep the road of dreams,

Peo - ple say that in the night,

The tur - tle will talk it seems,

The tur - tle will talk it seems.

72. GOODBYE OL' PAINT

ls mrd s₁   Cowboy Song

Good - bye   ol'   Paint,   I'm   a   leav - in'   Chey - enne,   *Fine*

My   foot   in   the   stir - rup,   my   po - ny   won't   stand,

I'm a   leav - in'   Chey - enne and   I'm   off   for   Mon - tan'.   *D.C.*

2. I'm a ridin' Ol' Paint and a leadin' Ol' Dan,
Goodbye little Annie. I'm off for Montan.

73. MISTER RABBIT

ls mrd s₁   Southern Folk Song

"Mis - ter   Rab - bit, Mis - ter   Rab - bit,   your   ears are might - y   long."

"Yes,   in - deed,   they're   put   on   wrong,"

Ev - ery   lit - tle   soul   must   shine,   shine,   shine,____

Ev - ery   lit - tle   soul   must   shine,____   shine,   shine!

2. "Mr. Rabbit, Mr. Rabbit, you leave my cabbage patch ! "
"Yes, indeed, don't hook that latch ! "

3. "Mr. Rabbit, Mr. Rabbit, your tail is mighty white ! "
"Yes, indeed, I'm gettin' out o' sight ! "

74. ALL NIGHT, ALL DAY

s mrd l₁ s₁   Spiritual

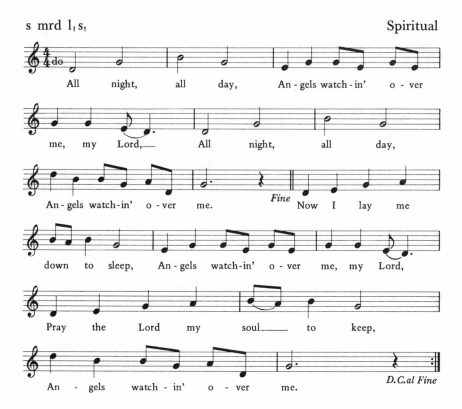

All night, all day, An - gels watch - in' o - ver
me, my Lord,— All night, all day,
An - gels watch-in' o - ver me. *Fine* Now I lay me
down to sleep, An - gels watch-in' o - ver me, my Lord,
Pray the Lord my soul___ to keep,
An - gels watch - in' o - ver me. *D.C. al Fine*

75. MY OLD HAMMER

s mrd l₁ s₁   Work Song

My old ham - mer___ shine-a like sil - ver,___
shine-a like gold, boys,___ yes shine-a like gold.___

2. Ain't no hammer, in-a this mountain,
   Shine-a like mine, boys, yes shine-a like mine.

3. I been working on-a this railroad,
   Four long years, boys, yes four long years.

76. O, JOHN THE RABBIT

s mrd l₁ s₁   Mississippi

O, John the Rab-bit, yes ma'm, Got a night-y hab-it, yes ma'm,

Jump-ing in my gar-den, yes ma'm, Cut-ting down my cab-bage, yes ma'm,

My sweet po-'ta - toes, yes ma'm, My fresh to - ma - toes, yes ma'm,

And if I live,— yes ma'm, To see next fall, yes ma'm,

I ain't gon-na have,— yes ma'm, No cot-ton at all, yes ma'm.

From *American Folk Songs for Children*. Reprinted by permission of Curtis Brown, Ltd. Copyright, 1948, by Ruth Crawford Seeger.

77. YONDER SHE COMES

s mrd l₁ s₁   Missouri

Yon - der she comes and it's how - dy, how -dy do, Oh,

Where have you been since the last that I met you?

2. Rise you up my lady, present to me your hand,
   I know you are a pretty girl, the prettiest in the land.

From *American Folk Songs for Children*. Reprinted by permission of Curtis Brown, Ltd. Copyright, 1948, by Ruth Crawford Seeger.

78. TOODALA

s mrd l, s,   Texas

Might-y pret-ty mo - tion, Too - da - la, too - da - la, too - da - la,

Might-y pret-ty mo - tion, Too - da - la, too - da-fa - la La - dy!

From *American Folk Songs for Children*. Reprinted by permission of Curtis Brown, Ltd. Copyright, 1948, by Ruth Crawford Seeger.

79. THE YOUNG MAN WHO WOULDN'T HOE CORN

s mrd l, s,   Frontier Ballad

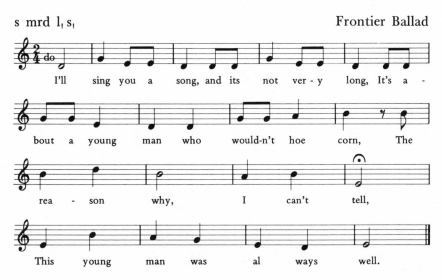

I'll sing you a song, and its not ver - y long, It's a -

bout a young man who would-n't hoe corn, The

rea - son why, I can't tell,

This young man was al ways well.

2. In September his corn was knee high,
   In October he laid it by,
   In November there came a great frost,
   And all this young man's corn was lost.

80. I'M GONNA SING

I'm gon - na sing when the spir - it says "Sing,"
I'm gon - na sing when the spir - it says "Sing."___
I'm gon - na sing when the spir - it says "Sing,"
And o - bey the spir - it of the Lord.

81. MARY HAD A BABY

Ma - ry had a ba - by, yes, Lord,
Ma - ry had a ba - by, yes, my Lord,
Ma - ry had a ba - by, yes, Lord, The
peo - ple keep a - com - in' but the train done gone.

2. Laid Him in a manger.

3. Shepherds came to see Him.

4. Angels sang His glory.

82. LONESOME VALLEY

ls mrd l₁ s₁ — Spiritual

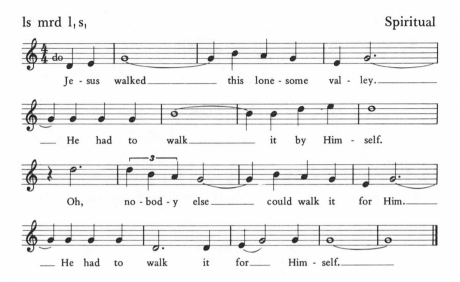

Je - sus walked_____ this lone - some val - ley._____

___ He had to walk_____ it by Him - self.

Oh, no - bod - y else_____ could walk it for Him._____

___ He had to walk it for___ Him - self._____

83. JENNY JENKINS

ls mrd l₁ s₁ — Appalachian

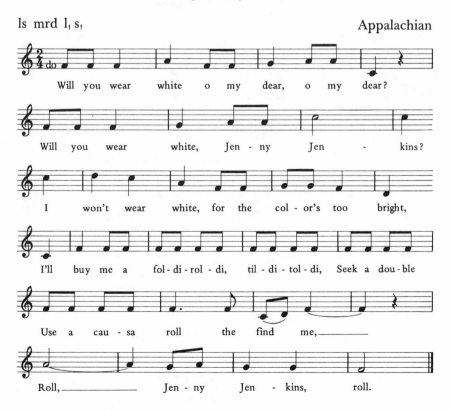

Will you wear white o my dear, o my dear?

Will you wear white, Jen - ny Jen - kins?

I won't wear white, for the col - or's too bright,

I'll buy me a fol - di - rol - di, til - di - tol - di, Seek a dou - ble

Use a cau - sa roll the find me,_____

Roll,_____ Jen - ny Jen - kins, roll.

84. THE SALLY BUCK

ls mrd l,s,   Appalachian

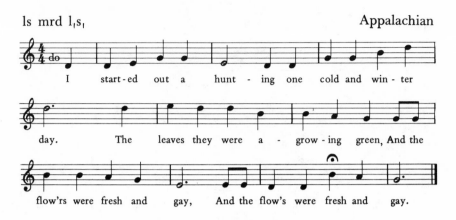

I start-ed out a hunt - ing one cold and win - ter

day. The leaves they were a - grow - ing green, And the

flow'rs were fresh and gay, And the flow's were fresh and gay.

2. I tracked the Sally buck all day,
   I tracked him through the snow;
   I tracked him through the waterside,
   And under he did go,
   And under he did go.

85. COTTON NEEDS PICKIN'

ls mrd l,s,   Work Song

Cot - ton needs pick - in' so bad,

Cot-ton needs pick-in' so bad,___ Cot-ton needs pick-in'

so bad I'm gon-na pick all o - ver this field.

Fine

Plant - ed this cot - ton in A - pril,

On the full of the moon. It's been a hot, dry

sum - mer, That's why it open-ed so soon.

D.C. al Fine

86. YONDER MOUNTAIN

ls mrd l₁s₁   Virginia

At the foot of yon-der moun-tain there runs a clear stream,

At the foot of yon - der moun-tain there lives .a fair queen.

She's hand-some, She's pro-per, and her ways are com - plete,

I_____ ask no bet-ter pas-time than to be with my sweet.

2. But why she won't have me I well understand;
   She wants some freeholder and I have no land
   I cannot maintain her on silver and gold,
   And all other fine things that my love's house should hold.

From *American Folk Tales and Songs* by Richard Chase. Dover Publications, Inc., New York, 1956. Reprinted through the permission of the publisher.

87. WAYFARING STRANGER

ls mrd l₁s₁   Spiritual

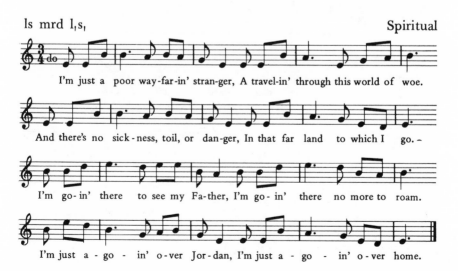

I'm just a poor way-far-in' stran-ger, A travel-in' through this world of woe.

And there's no sick-ness, toil, or dan-ger, In that far land to which I go. -

I'm go-in' there to see my Fa-ther, I'm go-in' there no more to roam.

I'm just a-go - in' o-ver Jor-dan, I'm just a - go - in' o-ver home.

88. TELL IT ON THE MOUNTAIN

ls mrd l,s,

Spiritual

When I was a seek-er, I sought both night and day,
I asked the Lord to help me, And He showed me the
way. Go tell it on the moun - tain,
O-ver the hills and ev - ery - where, Go tell it on the
moun - tain, That Je - sus Christ is born.

89. THE DEVIL'S QUESTIONS

ls mrd l,s,

Virginia

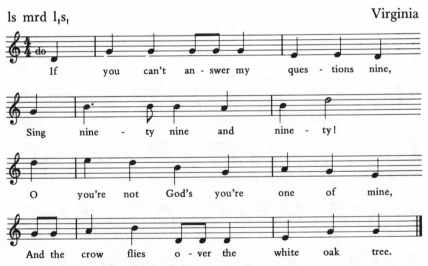

If you can't an - swer my ques - tions nine,
Sing nine - ty nine and nine - ty!
O you're not God's you're one of mine,
And the crow flies o - ver the white oak tree.

From *American Folk Tales and Songs* by Richard Chase. Dover Publications, Inc., New York, 1956. Reprinted through the permission of the publisher.

2. O what is higher than the tree ? And what is deeper than the sea ?

3. O heaven is higher than a tree, And love is deeper than the sea.

4. O what is whiter than the milk ? And what is softer than the silk ?

5. O snow is whiter than the milk, And down is softer than the silk.

6. O what is louder than the horn ? And what is sharper than the thorn ?

7. O thunder's louder than the horn, And hunger's sharper than the thorn.

8. What is heavier than the lead? And what is better than the bread?

9. Grief is heavier than the lead, God's blessing's better than the bread.

10. Now you have answered my questions nine, O you are God's, you're none of mine.

90. FROG WENT A-COURTIN'

ls mrd l₁s₁   Folk Song

91. WALK ALONG, JOHN

ls mrd l₁s₁   Oklahoma Traditional

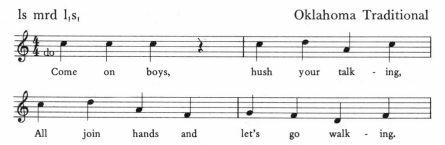

From *American Folk Songs for Children*. Reprinted by permission of Curtis Brown, Ltd. Copyright, 1948, by Ruth Crawford Seeger.

Walk a - long   John   with your   blue   shirt   on,

Walk a - long   John   with your   blue   shirt   on.

92. CHILD OF GOD

ls mrd l,s,   Spiritual

If   an - y bod - y   asks   you   who   I   am

Who   I   am   who   I   am   If

an - y bod - y   asks   you   who   I   am

Tell   him   I'm   a   child   of   God.

2. The little cradle rocks tonight in glory,
   Night in glory, night in glory.
   Little cradle rocks tonight in glory,
   Christmas child born in glory.

3. Peace on earth, Mary rock the cradle,
   Rock the cradle, rock the cradle.
   Peace on earth, Mary rock the cradle,
   Christ child born in glory.

4. The Christ child passing singing softly,
   Singing softly, singing softly,
   The Christ child passing singing softly,
   Christ child born in glory.

   (Repeat verse 1.)

93. CINDY

ls mrd l₁s₁

Southern Folk Song

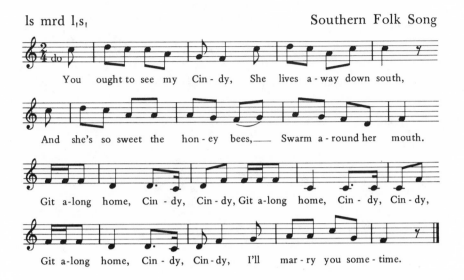

You ought to see my Cin - dy, She lives a - way down south,

And she's so sweet the hon - ey bees,—— Swarm a - round her mouth.

Git a-long home, Cin - dy, Cin - dy, Git a-long home, Cin - dy, Cin - dy,

Git a-long home, Cin - dy, Cin - dy, I'll mar - ry you some - time.

94. I HAD ME A BIRD

d' ls mrd

Traditional

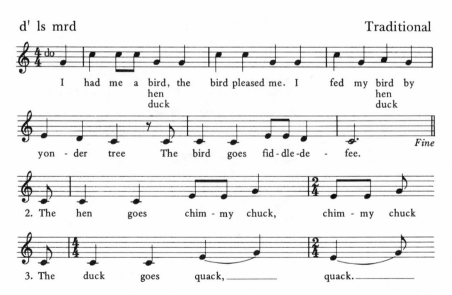

I had me a bird, the bird pleased me. I fed my bird by
    hen   hen
    duck   duck

yon - der tree The bird goes fid - dle-de - fee. *Fine*

2. The hen goes chim - my chuck, chim - my chuck

3. The duck goes quack,———— quack.————

95. WHEN THE TRAIN COMES ALONG

d' ls mrd   Spiritual

When the train comes a-long── When the train comes a - long──
I'll meet you at the sta - tion When the train comes a-long.
It may be ear - ly, It may be late,
But I'll meet you at the sta - tion When the train comes a - long.

96. THE GAMBLING SUITOR

d' ls mrd   Virginia

Sir I see you── come a - gain; pray tell me what it's for,
When I left you in── Bar - bour - ville,── I told you to come no
more.   I told you to come no── more.

2. Miss, I have a very fine house, newly built with pine,
   And you may have it at your command, if you will be my bride.

3. Sir I know it's very fine house, also a very fine yard,
   But who will stay at home with me when you're out playing cards?

From *American Folk Tales and Songs* by Richard Chase. Dover Publications, Inc., New York, 1956. Reprinted through the permission of the publisher.

97. BILLY CAME OVER THE MAIN WHITE OCEAN

d' ls mrd

Bil-ly came o-ver the main white o-cean, Bil-ly came o-ver the sea,
Bil-ly came down to my fa-ther's house, Bil-ly came a court-in' of
me, me, me, Bil-ly came a court-in' of me.

2. Go choose your pot of mother's gold
   And a pot of father's bees
   And to some far country we will go
   And it's married we will be, be, be,
   And it's married we will be.

98. THE MERRY GOLDEN TREE

d' ls mrdl, s,

Virginia

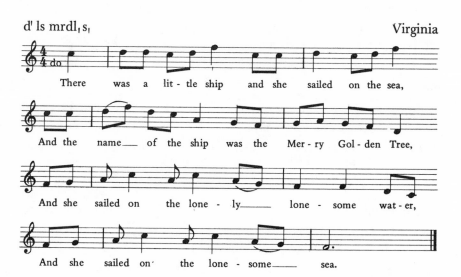

There was a lit-tle ship and she sailed on the sea,
And the name___ of the ship was the Mer-ry Gol-den Tree,
And she sailed on the lone-ly___ lone-some wat-er,
And she sailed on' the lone-some___ sea.

From *American Folk Tales and Songs* by Richard Chase. Dover Publications, Inc., New York, 1956. Reprinted through the permission of the publisher.

99. HOP UP, MY LADIES

r'd' ls mrd   Traditional

Hop up, my lad - ies, three in a row,
Hop up, my lad - ies, three in a row,
Hop up, my lad - ies, three in a row,
Don't mind the weath - er if the wind don't blow.

100. RAIN, COME WET ME

ın'r'd'ls mrd   Texas

Rain, come wet__ me, Sun, come dry__ me,
Keep a - way, pret - ty girls, Don't come nigh__ me!

From *American Folk Songs for Children*. Reprinted by permission of Curtis Brown, Ltd. Copyright. 1948, by Ruth Crawford Seeger.

101. RUN, CHILLUN, RUN

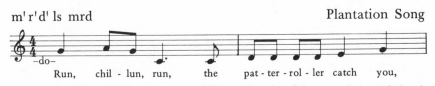

m'r'd' ls mrd   Plantation Song

Run, chil - lun, run, the pat - ter - rol - ler catch you,

From *American Folk Songs for Children*. Reprinted by permission of Curtis Brown, Ltd. Copyright, 1948, by Ruth Crawford Seeger.

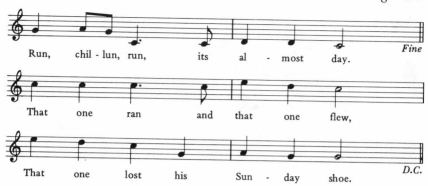

Run, chil - lun, run, its al - most day.

That one ran and that one flew,

That one lost his Sun - day shoe.

102. JUBA

fmrd

Traditional

Ju - ba this and Ju - ba that, Ju - ba killed a yel - low cat,

Ju - ba up and Ju - ba down, Ju - ba run - ning all a - round.

From *American Folk Songs for Children*. Reprinted by permission of Curtis Brown, Ltd. Copyright, 1948, by Ruth Crawford Seeger.

103. OLD AUNT KATE

sfmrd

American Folk Song

Old Aunt Kate she bake a cake, She bake it 'hind the gar - den gate,

She sift the meal, give me the dust, She bake the bread, give me the crust,

She eat the meat, give me the skin, And that's the way she took me in.

From *American Folk Songs for Children*. Reprinted by permission of Curtis Brown, Ltd. Copyright, 1948, by Ruth Crawford Seeger.

104. HANGING OUT THE LINEN CLOTHES

fmrd   American Folk Song

'Twas on a Monday morn - ing, the first I saw my darl - ing,

A - wash-ing out the linen cloth-es, a - wash-ing out the linen cloth-es.

2. Tuesday a-hanging out   5. Friday a-mending of

3. Wednesday a-talking in   6. Saturday a-folding of

4. Thursday a-running of   7. Sunday a-wearing of

From *American Folk Songs for Children*. Reprinted by permission of Curtis Brown, Ltd. Copyright, 1948, by Ruth Crawford Seeger.

105. WHISTLE, DAUGHTER, WHISTLE

sfmrd   Southern Folk Song

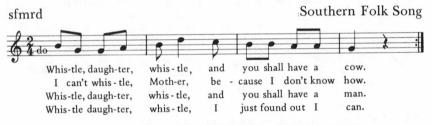

Whis-tle, daugh-ter,   whis-tle,   and   you shall have a   cow.
I can't whis-tle,   Moth-er,   be - cause I don't know how.
Whis-tle, daugh-ter,   whis-tle,   and   you shall have a   man.
Whis-tle daugh-ter,   whis-tle,   I   just found out I   can.

106. SOMETIMES I FEEL LIKE A MOURNING DOVE

sfmrd   Southern

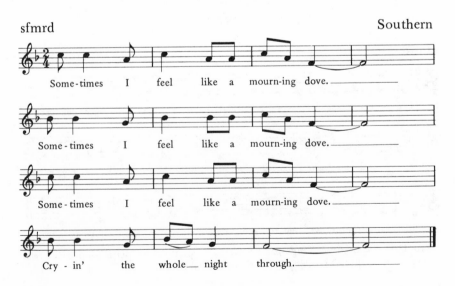

Some-times   I   feel   like   a   mourn-ing   dove.___

Some - times   I   feel   like   a   mourn-ing   dove.___

Some - times   I   feel   like   a   mourn-ing   dove.___

Cry - in'   the   whole___ night   through.___

107. JOYFUL, JOYFUL

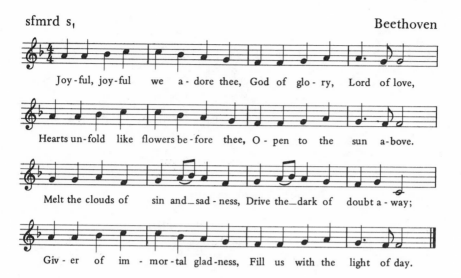

sfmrd s,   Beethoven

Joy-ful, joy-ful   we a-dore thee, God of glo-ry,   Lord of love,

Hearts un-fold   like flowers be-fore thee, O-pen to the   sun a-bove.

Melt the clouds of   sin and—sad-ness, Drive the—dark of   doubt a-way;

Giv-er   of   im-mor-tal glad-ness, Fill us   with the   light of day.

108. DA PACEM DOMINE

sfmrd   Canon, Latin, 1600

1   2

Da   pa-cem   Do-mi-ne,   da   pa-cem

Do-mi-ne   in di-e-bus   Nos-tris.

109. ORANGES, LEMONS

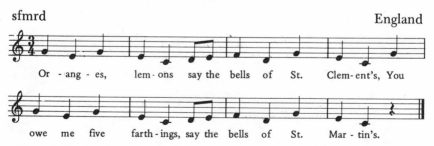

sfmrd   England

Or-ang-es,   lem-ons   say the bells of St.   Clem-ent's, You

owe   me   five   farth-ings, say the bells   of St.   Mar-tin's.

From *Sally Go Round the Sun* by Edith Fowke. Copyright © 1969 by Mc-Clelland & Stewart, Ltd. Reprinted by permission of Doubleday & Company, Inc. and the Canadian publishers, McClelland and Stewart Limited, Toronto.

110. CRADLE HYMN

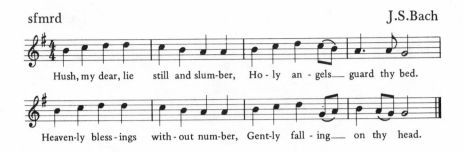

Hush, my dear, lie still and slum-ber, Ho - ly an - gels — guard thy bed.

Heaven-ly bless - ings with - out num-ber, Gent-ly fall - ing — on thy head.

111. STARS SHININ'

By'n bye, By'n bye. Stars shin-ing

Num - ber, num - ber one, num - ber two, Num - ber three,

Good lawd, by'n bye, by'n bye, Good lawd, By'n bye.

From *American Folk Songs for Children*. Reprinted by permission of Curtis Brown, Ltd. Copyright, 1948, by Ruth Crawford Seeger.

112. CHRISTMAS GREETINGS

Good bless all good friends here, A mer - ry, mer - ry

Christ - mas and a Hap - py New Year!

113. JIMMY ROSE HE WENT TO TOWN

lsfmrd   Southern

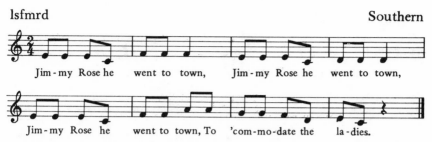

Jim-my Rose he   went to town,   Jim-my Rose he   went to town,

Jim-my Rose he   went to town, To 'com-mo-date the   la-dies.

From *American Folk Songs for Children*. Reprinted by permission of Curtis Brown, Ltd. Copyright, 1948, by Ruth Crawford Seeger.

114. IT RAINED A MIST

lsfmrd   Virginia

It   rained   a mist,   it   rained a mist,   It   rained all o - ver the

town, town, town,   It   rained__ all   o - ver   the   town.____

From *American Folk Songs for Children*. Reprinted by permission of Curtis Brown, Ltd. Copyright, 1948, by Ruth Crawford Seeger.

115. I SAW THREE SHIPS

lsfmrd   England

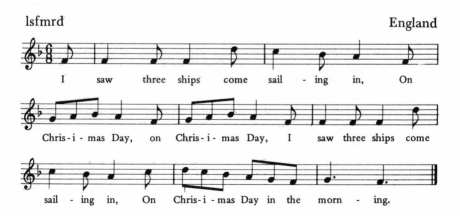

I   saw   three ships   come   sail - ing   in,   On

Chris-i - mas Day,   on   Chris- i- mas Day,   I   saw three ships come

sail - ing in,   On   Chris-i - mas Day in the   morn - ing.

116. TURN, CINNAMON, TURN

lsfmrd   Florida

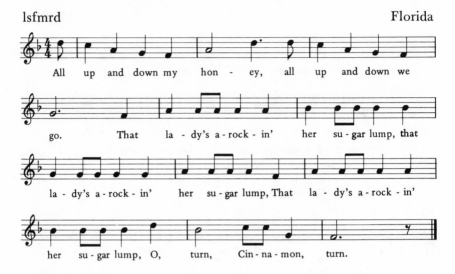

All up and down my hon - ey, all up and down we go. That la - dy's a - rock - in' her su - gar lump, that la - dy's a - rock - in' her su - gar lump, That la - dy's a - rock - in' her su - gar lump, O, turn, Cin - na - mon, turn.

From *Games and Songs of American Children* by William Wells Newell. Dover Publications, Inc., New York, 1963.

117. WATER, WATER, WILDFLOWERS

lsfmrd   New York

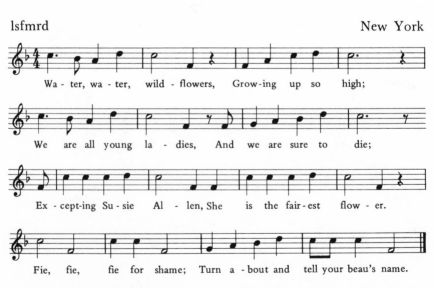

Wa - ter, wa - ter, wild - flowers, Grow-ing up so high; We are all young la - dies, And we are sure to die; Ex - cept-ing Su - sie Al - len, She is the fair - est flow - er. Fie, fie, fie for shame; Turn a - bout and tell your beau's name.

From *Games and Songs of American Children* by William Wells Newell. Dover Publications, Inc., New York, 1963.

118. THIS OLD MAN

lsfmrd   New York

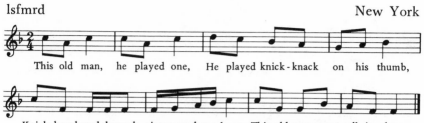

This old man, he played one, He played knick-knack on his thumb,

Knick-knack pad-dy wack, give your dog a bone, This old man came roll-ing home.

2. This old man, he played two, he played knick-knack on his shoe.

3. This old man, he played three, he played knick-knack on his knee.

4. This old man, he played four, he played knick-knack on the floor.

5. This old man, he played five, he played knick-knack on his hives.

From *American Folk Songs for Children*. Reprinted by permission of Curtis Brown, Ltd. Copyright, 1948, by Ruth Crawford Seeger.

119. FIRE DOWN BELOW

lsfmrd   American Folk Song

There's fire in the low-er deck, Fire down be-low,

Fire in the main well, The cap-tain did-n't know.

Fire! Fire! Fire down be-low.

It's fetch a pail of wa-ter, girls! There's fire down be-low.

From *American Folk Songs for Children*. Reprinted by permission of Curtis Brown, Ltd. Copyright, 1948, by Ruth Crawford Seeger.

120. THE OLD CHISHOLM TRAIL

lsfmrd

Cowboy Song

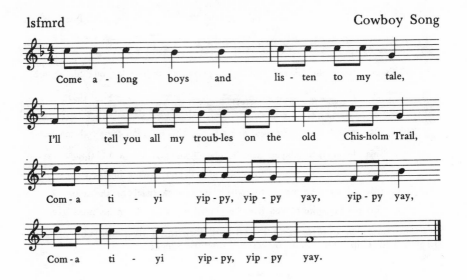

Come a - long boys and lis - ten to my tale,

I'll tell you all my troub-les on the old Chis-holm Trail,

Com - a ti - yi yip - py, yip - py yay, yip - py yay,

Com - a ti - yi yip - py, yip - py yay.

121. BROTHER JOHN

lsfmrd s₁

French Round

Are you sleep-ing? Are you sleep-ing? Bro - ther John, Bro - ther John,

Morn-ing bells are ring-ing, Morn-ing bells are ring-ing, Ding ding dong, Ding ding dong.

122. JOSEPH DEAREST, JOSEPH MILD

lsfmrd   German

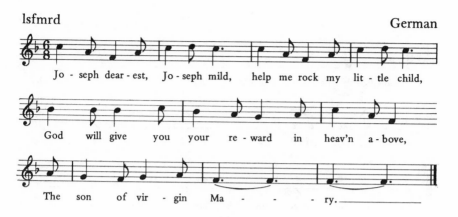

Jo - seph dear - est, Jo - seph mild, help me rock my lit - tle child,

God will give you your re - ward in heav'n a - bove,

The son of vir - gin Ma - ry.

123. NEW RIVER TRAIN

lsfmrd   American Folk Song

I'm rid - in' that New Riv - er Train,

I'm rid - in' that New Riv - er Train,

Same old train that brought me here, gon - na

take me back home a - gain.

124. FIDDLE-DE-DE

lsfmrd

English Folk Song

Fid-dle-de-de, Fid-dle-de-de, the fly has mar-ried the bum-ble-bee. Says the fly says he will you mar-ry me, and live with me sweet bum-ble-bee? Fid-dle-de-de, Fid-dle-de-de, the fly has mar-ried the bum-ble-bee.

125. BARLEY, BARLEY, BUCKWHEAT, STRAW

lsfmrd

Southern

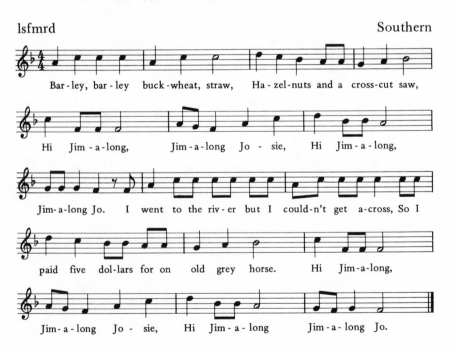

Bar-ley, bar-ley buck-wheat, straw, Ha-zel-nuts and a cross-cut saw, Hi Jim-a-long, Jim-a-long Jo-sie, Hi Jim-a-long, Jim-a-long Jo. I went to the riv-er but I could-n't get a-cross, So I paid five dol-lars for on old grey horse. Hi Jim-a-long, Jim-a-long Jo-sie, Hi Jim-a-long Jim-a-long Jo.

126. PUNCHINELLO

d' lsfmrd
Traditional

Look who is here, Pun-chi-nel-lo, fun-ny fel-low!

Look who is here, Pun-chi-nel-lo, fun-ny, do!

2. What can you do, Punchinello, funny fellow?
3. We'll do it, too, Punchinello, funny fellow.

127. PAUPER SUM EGO

m'r'd'tls d
Latin Canon

Pau-per sum e-go. Ni-hil ha-be-o. Cor me-um da-bo.

128. RISE UP, O FLAME

l mrdt₁l₁
Praetorius

Rise up, O flame____ by__ thy__ light glow-ing.

Show to us beau-ty__ vi__sion__and joy.

129. THE BIRCH TREE

mrdt₁l₁
Russian Folk Song

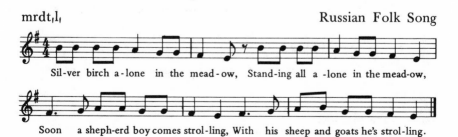

Sil-ver birch a-lone in the mead-ow, Stand-ing all a-lone in the mead-ow,

Soon a shep-herd boy comes strol-ling, With his sheep and goats he's strol-ling.

130. LAUGHING SONG

dt₁l₁s₁   Swedish

Ha ha ha!   He he he!   An-der-son and Pe-ter-son and
Jen - son and me.   Ha   ha   ha!   He   he   he!
Sing - ing all   to - geth - er,   sing - ing   mer - ri - ly.

131. HEY, HO, NOBODY HOME

mrdt₁l₁s₁m₁   English Round

Hey, Ho!   No - bod-y home,   Meat nor drink nor   mon-ey have I none,
Yet,   I will   be   mer - ry, ver-y mer-ry, Hey,   Ho!   No-bod-y home.

132. I'S THE B'Y

sfmrdt₁s₁   Newfoundland

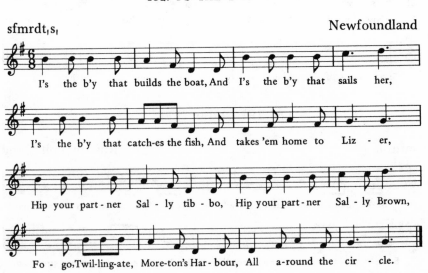

I's   the b'y   that builds the boat, And   I's   the b'y   that   sails   her,
I's   the b'y   that catch-es the fish,   And   takes 'em home to   Liz - er,
Hip your part - ner   Sal - ly tib - bo,   Hip your part - ner   Sal - ly Brown,
Fo - go, Twil-ling-ate, More-ton's Har - bour, All   a-round the cir - cle.

133. MARCHING DOWN THE LEVEE

ls mrdt,l,s,   Southern

We're march - ing down the lev - ee, We're march - ing down the lev - ee,

We're march - ing down the lev - ee, To old Shi - loh.

Swing 'em on the cor - ner, too -dle - la, Too -dle - la, too - dle -la,

Swing 'em on the cor - ner, too - dle - la, Too- dle - la - da - ay.

134. NIGHTTIME

Hungarian Folk Song
Words:Sr.Kathleen Dalton

mrdt, ,

Sails in the sun - set gleam in the sha - dows,

Lil - ies and jas - mine per - fume the night - time,

All the birds are sleep - ing in their nest - ed rush - es,

And the stars are watch-ing while the world is dream - ing.

135. BLOW, YE WINDS IN THE MORNING

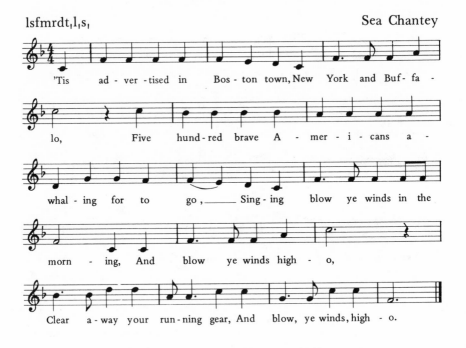

lsfmrdt₁l₁s₁   Sea Chantey

'Tis ad-ver-tised in Bos-ton town, New York and Buf-fa-
lo, Five hund-red brave A-mer-i-cans a-
whal-ing for to go,___ Sing-ing blow ye winds in the
morn-ing, And blow ye winds high-o,
Clear a-way your run-ning gear, And blow, ye winds, high-o.

136. THIS LITTLE GOSPEL LIGHT

d' tlsfmrd   Spiritual

This lit-tle gos-pel light of mine, I'm gon-na make it shine,
This lit-tle gos-pel light of mine, I'm gon-na make it shine,
This lit-tle gos-pel light of mine, I'm gon-na make it shine,
Make it shine, make it shine, make it shine.___

137. VIVA LA MUSICA

sfmrdt₁l₁s₁f₁   Praetorius Canon

Vi - va, Vi - va la   mu - si - ca,   Vi - va, Vi - va la
mu - si - ca,   Vi - va   la   mu - si - ca.

138. THE STREETS OF LAREDO

sfmrdt₁s₁   Texas

As   I___ walked   out   in   the   streets of La - re - do,   as
I   walked   out   in   La - re - do   one   day.
I   spied   a cow   punch-er wrapped   up   in   white   lin - en
Wrapped up   in white   lin - en   as   cold   as   the   clay.

2. Oh, beat the drum slowly, and play the fife lowly,
   Play the dead march as you carry me along;
   Take me to the green valley, there lay the sod o'er me,
   For I'm a young cowboy and I know I've done wrong.

139. ST. ANTHONY'S CHORALE

fmrdt,l,s,   Franz Joseph Haydn

Fine

D.C. al Fine

140. SHENANDOAH

dtlsfmrd s,

Virginia

Oh, Shen-an-doah, I long to   hear you, A - way you roll-ing

riv - er,   Oh,   Shen-an-doah,   I long to   hear you.

A - way, I'm bound to   go,   'Cross the wide Mis - sour - i.

141. SOLDIER, SOLDIER, WILL YOU MARRY ME?

sfmrdt,l,s,   American Folk Song

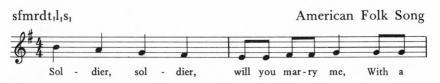

Sol - dier,   sol - dier,   will you mar-ry me,   With a

From *Games and Songs of American Children* by William Wells Newell.
Dover Publications, Inc., New York, 1963.

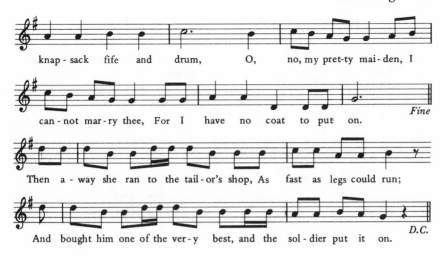

knap - sack fife and drum, O, no, my pret-ty mai- den, I

can - not mar - ry thee, For I have no coat to put on.

Fine

Then a - way she ran to the tail - or's shop, As fast as legs could run;

And bought him one of the ver - y best, and the sol - dier put it on.

D.C.

At each verse another article of clothing is mentioned: gloves, hat, boots, etc.

On the last verse the soldier sings:

'O, no, my pretty maid, I cannot marry thee,

For I have a good wife at home!

142. IN THE BLEAK MIDWINTER

Words: Christine Rossetti

lsfmrdt₁

Music: Gustav Holst

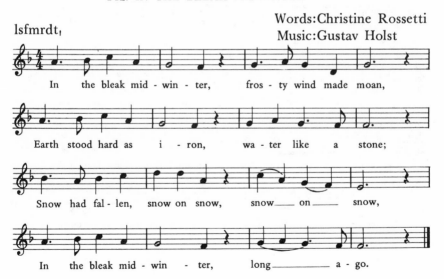

In the bleak mid - win - ter, fros - ty wind made moan,

Earth stood hard as i - ron, wa - ter like a stone;

Snow had fal - len, snow on snow, snow___ on ___ snow,

In the bleak mid - win - ter, long_____ a - go.

143. JOHNNY HAS GONE FOR A SOLDIER

dtls mrd

Revolutionary War Song

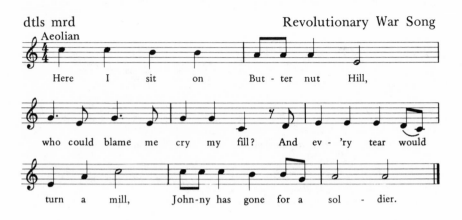

Here I sit on But - ter nut Hill, who could blame me cry my fill? And ev - 'ry tear would turn a mill, John-ny has gone for a sol - dier.

144. BLUE MOUNTAIN LAKE

ls mrdt,l,

New York

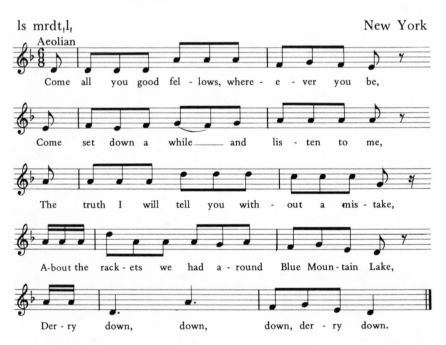

Come all you good fel - lows, where - e - ver you be, Come set down a while and lis - ten to me, The truth I will tell you with - out a mis - take, A-bout the rack - ets we had a - round Blue Moun - tain Lake, Der - ry down, down, down, der - ry down.

145. WHEN JESUS WEPT

lsfmrdt₁l₁s₁ m₁   William Billings

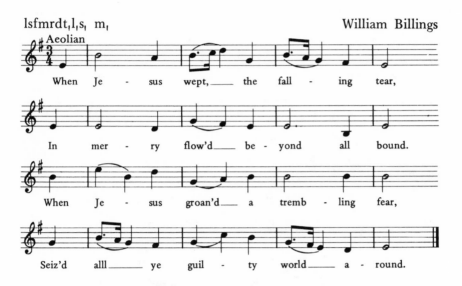

When Je - sus wept,___ the fall - ing tear,

In mer - ry flow'd___ be - yond all bound.

When Je - sus groan'd___ a tremb - ling fear,

Seiz'd alll___ ye guil - ty world___ a - round.

146. PAT WORKS ON THE RAILWAY

rdtls₁ f₁ m₁   Work Song

In eight - een hund-red and for - ty one I put me cor-du-roy

britch - es on, I put me cor-du-roy britch - es on to

work up - on the rail - way. Fill - a - mi - oo - re -

oo - re - ay, Fill - a - mi - oo - re - oo - re - ay,

Fill - a - mi - oo - re - oo - re - ay, To work up-on the rail - way.

147. O COME, EMMANUEL

From an 18th Century
French Mass Book

sfmrdt,l,s,
Aeolian

O come, O come Em - man - - u - el,

And ran - som cap - tive Is - - ra - el;

That mourns in lone - ly ex - ile here,

Un - til the son of God ap - pear.

Re - joice, re - joice, Em - man - - u - el,

Shall come to thee, O Is - - ra - el.

148. BOUND FOR THE PROMISED LAND

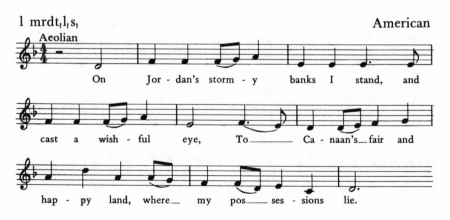

American

l mrdt,l,s,
Aeolian

On Jor - dan's storm - y banks I stand, and

cast a wish - ful eye, To Ca - naan's fair and

hap - py land, where my pos - ses - sions lie.

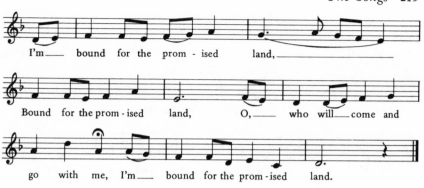

I'm bound for the prom - ised land,

Bound for the prom - ised land, O, who will come and

go with me, I'm bound for the prom - ised land.

149. OLD JOE CLARK

Mixolydian
ta lsfmrd

Tennessee

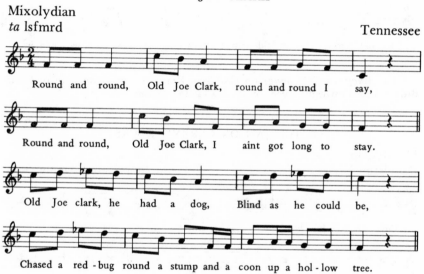

Round and round, Old Joe Clark, round and round I say,

Round and round, Old Joe Clark, I aint got long to stay.

Old Joe clark, he had a dog, Blind as he could be,

Chased a red - bug round a stump and a coon up a hol - low tree.

150. POOR OLD CROW

Mixolydian
d *ta* sfmrd

Virginia

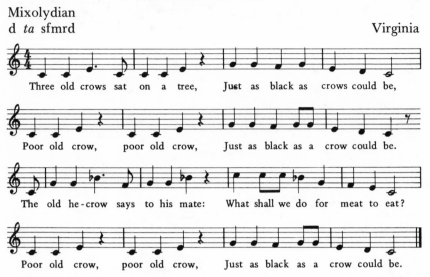

Three old crows sat on a tree, Just as black as crows could be,

Poor old crow, poor old crow, Just as black as a crow could be.

The old he-crow says to his mate: What shall we do for meat to eat?

Poor old crow, poor old crow, Just as black as a crow could be.

From *American Folk Songs for Children*. Reprinted by permission of Curtis Brown, Ltd. Copyright, 1948, by Ruth Crawford Seeger.

151. THE JAM ON GERRY'S ROCKS

Mixolydian
d *ta* lsfmrd

American Logging Song

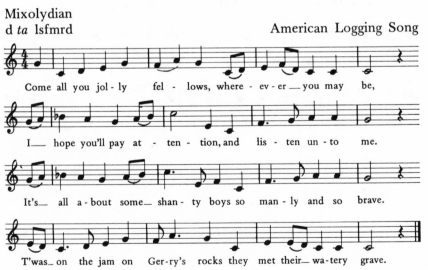

Come all you jol-ly fel-lows, where-ev-er __ you may be,

I __ hope you'll pay at-ten-tion, and lis-ten un-to me.

It's __ all a-bout some __ shan-ty boys so man-ly and so brave.

T'was __ on the jam on Ger-ry's rocks they met their __ wa-tery grave.

152. SWEET WATER ROLLING

sfmrdt₁ *ta* l₁s₁   South Carolina

Sweet wa - ter roll - ing, sweet wa-ter roll.

Roll-ing from the foun - tain, sweet wa - ter roll.

153. HAUL AWAY, JOE

Dorian   American
ls *fi* mr l₁   Sea Chantey

When I was just a ti - ny lad my dear old moth-er told___ me,

Way - haul a - way we'll haul a - way, Joe,

That if I nev - er kissed a girl my lips would go all mould - y. .

Way, haul a - way, we'll haul a - way, Joe.

154. AS I ROVED OUT

Dorian

s *fi* mrdt, l,

Newfoundland

As I roved out one fine sum-mer's eve - ning,

To view the flowers and to take the ___ air,

'Twas there I spied a ten - der ___ moth - er,

Talk - in' to her ___ daught - er ___ fair.

2. A sailor boy thinks all for to wander,
   And he will prove your overthrow.
   O daughter, you're better to wed with a farmer,
   For to sea he'll never go.

155. AH POOR BIRD

l *si* mrdt l

English Canon

Ah poor bird, take your flight,

Far a - bove the sor - rows of this sad night.

2. Ah poor bird, as you fly,
   Can you see the dawn of tomorrow's sky?

156. GO DOWN, MOSES

mrdtl *si* m   Spiritual

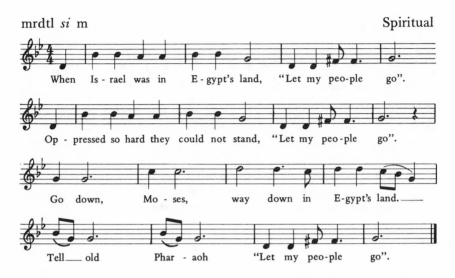

When Is-rael was in E-gypt's land, "Let my peo-ple go".

Op-pressed so hard they could not stand, "Let my peo-ple go".

Go down, Mo-ses, way down in E-gypt's land.——

Tell—— old Phar-aoh "Let my peo-ple go".

157. MAM'ZELLE ZIZI

s mrdtl *si*   Creole

Don't you cry Mam'-zelle Zi-zi, Don't you cry Mam'-zelle Zi-zi,

Tears are ver-y sad to see, And your sights bring, mi-se-ry.

I will give you flow-ers fair, Silk-en rib-bons for your hair,

Pret-ty pearls so white and rare, And a ring for you to wear.

158. BY THE WATERS BABYLON

dt *ta* l *si* sfmrd l,   Anon. Canon

By the__ wa-ters,   by the__ wa-ters,   by the__ wa-ters   Ba - by-lon,

We   sat down and   wept,__   we   wept,__   we   wept,____   When

we   re-mem-bered, we   re-mem-bered, we   re-mem-bered   Zi - on.

Alphabetical Index of Songs